I0459304

ONE YEAR FROM YESTERDAY

No More Short-Lived Resolutions!
Your Science-Backed Guided Journal
That Actually Helps to Build Better Habits
and Lets You Reach Your Goals
- All Year Long!

COPYRIGHT

© 2025 KOMMOR Consulting

All rights reserved.

No part of this publication may be reproduced, stored in a retrieval system, or transmitted in any form or by any means — electronic, mechanical, photocopying, recording, or otherwise — without the prior written permission of the publisher, except for brief quotations used in reviews or scholarly works.

This book is intended for personal use and inspiration. It is not a substitute for professional counseling or therapy. The author and publisher disclaim any liability arising from the use or misuse of the content within.

Written by Alexandra Estroff for KOMMOR Consulting

www.kommor-consulting.com

Cover design & Illustrations by the author.

First Edition, 2025

TABLE OF CONTENTS

BLOOM SEASON

HARVEST SEASON

Introduction

The Problem with Traditional Goal-Setting

Here's what typically happens with resolutions, particularly New Year's ones: January arrives, you feel inspired, and set ambitious goals. Week 1 and 2 go great. In Week 3, the novelty starts to wear off. By the time the second month starts, life throws in a little chaos — you miss a day, then two, then a week. By Week 6, momentum is gone, priorities forgotten, and goals abandoned.

Data backs it up: **80% of New Year's resolutions fail by February**. By Week 12, only 8% of people are still actively working toward their goals. But the problem isn't you. It's the outdated approach: Traditional goal-setting assumes motivation is consistent, life is predictable, and willpower is infinite. None of that is true.

So, what actually works? Systems, structure, and support — not just at the start, but steadily, through the entire journey.

Why This Book Exists — And What Makes It Truly Different

Most goal-setting books tell you to dream big, make a plan, and hustle until you reach the finish line. They hand you blank pages sprinkled with inspirational quotes and expect you to fill them with determination alone. At first, this might be motivating. Very soon, though, real life steps in. Your goals quietly retreat to the back of a drawer, gathering dust, until you find them around the next holiday season when bringing out the decorations and wrapping paper again. This book is different - I promise!

I've lived that loop—year after year. Hi, my name is Alexandra, founder of KOMMOR Consulting. I have dedicated my mission to supporting ambitious people like you in finding clarity, strengthening interpersonal connections, and building sustainable momentum. The KOMMOR approach is rooted in emotional intelligence, **translating scientific research into easily applicable, life-proof action steps**. I wrote *One Year from Yesterday* because I never quite found any resource like it during all these years of personal development. **It's the book I wish I had had 15 years ago.**

Here's what sets it apart: It doesn't assume you need more motivation or bigger goals. And it definitely doesn't rely on fluffy prompts that sound good on social media but lack depth to actually add value to your journey. Instead, *One Year from Yesterday* gives you structure, support, and science-backed (yet real-life suitable) strategies to help you **turn meaningful intentions into sustainable action** — week by week, season by season.

This isn't just a book. It's your companion for the next 52 weeks — **no matter if you start on January 1st, take your birthday as the kick-off point, or a random Tuesday, just because the time feels right.** This guide meets you where you are, every single time.

Some weeks you'll feel unstoppable. Others, you might feel exhausted. This book adjusts to both with compassion and clarity.

Because it's grounded in behavioral science, **every chapter equips you with research on habit formation, motivation, and identity shifts that help you understand and recognize your patterns.** You'll learn to use them in a way that works for you, not against you. While *One Year from Yesterday* won't tell you who to become by Week 52, **it will help you keep going toward your very own, personal goals—even when life gets unpredictable. Especially then.**

How This Book Works

The Four Seasons of Growth

Change doesn't happen all at once — it unfolds in phases. That's why this book is structured around four 12-week "seasons," each reflecting a natural rhythm of transformation.

Seed Season (Weeks 1-12): Planting Intention. You're just beginning. This season helps you build structure while your motivation is still fresh. You'll learn how to attach rituals to existing habits, create an environment that supports you, and move through your first dip in energy with care. By the end, your routines will be consistent — not yet automatic, but rooted.

Sprout Season (Weeks 14-25): Nurturing Habits. Welcome to the messy middle — the part where motivation fades and progress feels slow. This is where most people give up. But not you. Here, you'll normalize setbacks, stay the course, and protect your momentum. By the end, your habits will begin to feel second nature.

Bloom Season (Weeks 27-38): Embodying Growth. This is the turning point. You're no longer forcing change — you're living it. This season is about owning your progress, making peace with discomfort, and noticing how far you've come. By the end, you'll feel yourself becoming the person you once imagined.

Harvest Season (Weeks 40-51): Integrating & Sustaining. You're gathering the fruits of your work. You'll reflect on what worked, release what no longer serves you, and prepare for what's next. This season is about sustaining growth without striving — and knowing you've already arrived.

Milestone Reflections (Week 13, 26, 39, 52): At the close of each season, you'll pause. These milestone check-ins help you notice progress, course-correct when needed, and celebrate what's unfolding — even if you can't always see it day to day.

What to Expect

Each week offers research-backed insights, practical tools, and a focused theme to help you stay consistent — even when motivation wavers. You bring the goals; this book brings the structure, science, and steady support.

One Year from Yesterday is for anyone ready to finally follow through — whether your goals are personal, professional, creative, or health-related — this journey honors the truth that real change isn't linear. Some weeks will feel effortless, others like a climb. That's okay. That's the process. We'll work through it together. One small, steady step at a time.

Before diving into Week 1, complete the prep-work on the following page:

- _Define 2–3 meaningful goals_
- _Break them into quarterly milestones_
- _Set your weekly rituals for the first 12 weeks._

Then, every week, track your rituals and read only the one corresponding chapter.

After each season, you will complete your milestone reflection and define the rituals for the coming 12 weeks. Don't worry, you don't have to memorize all of this right now. We will address each step when it's time. For now, let's get started.

PREP-WORK
SETTING YOURSELF UP FOR THE SUCCESS AHEAD

Before diving into Week 1, you want to get clear on three things:

1. **What are your 2-3 goals for this year?**
2. **What are your quarterly milestones for each goal?**
3. **What weekly rituals will move you toward those milestones?**

Let's break this down step by step.

STEP 1: CHOOSE YOUR 2-3 GOALS

You probably already have an idea in mind — something you want to accomplish, or someone you're ready to become. This next step is about turning those ideas into clear, meaningful goals that will guide your year. You don't need ten goals. In fact, the fewer, the better. Choosing 2–3 that truly matter allows you to focus your energy, build real habits, and stay connected to what you're working toward.

Choosing Your Goals: Three Guiding Questions

To help you choose, consider these three areas of life:

- **How do I want to feel in my body and mind?**
  → *Health, energy, mental clarity, physical strength, stress management, ...*
- **How do I want to grow professionally or creatively?**
  → *Career advancement, skill development, side projects, creative expression, ...*
- **How do I want to connect with others and myself?**
  → *Relationships, community, self-awareness, quality time, ...*

You don't need to pick one from each category. These are simply prompts to help you think broadly about what matters most right now.

Identity-Based Goals vs. Outcome Goals

Here's an important distinction that will shape how you approach your year:

Outcome goals	Identity-based goals
→ Focus on **what you want to achieve:**	→ Focus on **who you want to become**:
• *"Lose 20 pounds"*	• *"Someone who prioritizes health"*
• *"Pass B2 Level French"*	• *"Someone who leads with confidence"*
• *"Get a promotion"*	• *"Someone who makes intentional*
• *"Save $15,000"*	*financial choices"*

Both are valid. However, **identity-based goals tend to be more sustainable** because they're about building a new version of yourself, not just checking off a result. Choose what feels right for you. Some people thrive with clear outcome targets. Others prefer the flexibility of identity-based goals. You can even mix both.

Step 2: Break Each Goal Into Quarterly Milestones

Now that you have your 2-3 goals, it's time to break them down into manageable pieces. A year is long and unpredictable. Twelve weeks are much more manageable.

Ask yourself: What does meaningful progress look like every three months?

You're not committing to a fixed path — you're outlining a direction. You'll refine and recalibrate at the end of each season, once you've seen what actually works for you.

Goal Example 1: Feel healthier and more energized
- *25% Milestone: Establish a consistent movement routine (3x/week)*
- *50% Milestone: Add strength training and improve sleep habits*
- *75% Milestone: Focus on nutrition and meal planning*
- *100% Milestone: Maintain all habits and reflect on what feels sustainable long-term*

Goal Example 2: Grow my career and develop leadership skills
- *25% Milestone: Complete one professional development course*
- *50% Milestone: Lead one high-visibility project at work*
- *75% Milestone: Build relationships with 3 mentors or sponsors*
- *100% Milestone: Apply for promotion or new role*

Goal Example 3: Stay connected to the people who matter most
- *25% Milestone: Schedule regular check-ins with family (weekly calls)*
- *50% Milestone: Plan one meaningful gathering with friends each month*
- *75% Milestone: Reconnect with 3 people I've lost touch with*
- *100% Milestone: Reflect on relationships and set intentions for the next year*

Notice how each quarter builds on the last. You're not trying to do everything at once— you're layering progress over time.

Step 3: Define Your Weekly Rituals

This is where real change happens: through small, repeated actions. For the first 25% milestone, choose 1–3 small, weekly rituals that will support your progress.

When it comes to defining the weekly rituals, there are two helpful ways to approach this— and the best one depends on your goal and where you're starting from.

- *The first is **steady repetition**: you choose one ritual and repeat it each week for the entire season. This works well for building new habits because consistency helps the behavior become automatic over time.*
- *The second is **progressive increase**: you start small and gradually build over the weeks, increasing time, intensity, or frequency as you go. This approach suits goals that benefit from growth and flexibility, especially if you're building on an existing skill.*

Not sure which to choose? Ask yourself:

- *Am I starting from scratch or refining something?*
- *Do I thrive with routine, or do I prefer variety?*

There's no right or wrong — just what works for you right now. If steady repetition brings ease, go with that. If you need variety to stay engaged, try a progressive rhythm.

Either way, the goal is to create rituals that support your growth — not overwhelm it.

Your Goal-Setting Template

Goal # 1:

25% Milestone

Weekly Rituals
→
→
→

50% Milestone

75% Milestone

100% Milestone

Goal # 2:

25% Milestone

Weekly Rituals
→
→
→

50% Milestone

75% Milestone

100% Milestone

GOAL # 3:

....

25% Milestone

....

Weekly Rituals

→

→

→

....

50% Milestone

....

75% Milestone

....

100% Milestone

....

Final Preparation

Before you turn to Week 1, pause and really take in what you've just done. You've chosen goals that truly matter to you. You've broken them into meaningful milestones. You've designed weekly rituals to support your growth — not just in theory, but in practice.

Most people never get this far. They dream, they plan vaguely, they hope—but they don't build structure. You have.

Now, close your eyes for a few seconds. Picture yourself a year from now—living as the person who followed through. Who actually achieved these goals. Feel it. The pride. The peace. The strength. The quiet joy of being someone who finally kept going.

Capture that feeling. Let it stay with you. Return to it whenever you hit a rough patch.

One year from yesterday, your future self will thank you for what you're doing right now.

You're ready. Turn the page. Week 1 has already begun.

WEEK 1: BUILDING ON WHAT ALREADY WORKS
THE POWER OF HABIT STACKING

Welcome to Week 1. You've done the prep-work. You've chosen your goals, defined your milestones, and clarified your rituals. Now comes the most important question: how do you actually make these new behaviors stick? You don't need to create motivation from scratch. You need to attach your new rituals to the habits you already have.

The Research: Habit Stacking and Contextual Cues

Psychologist Wendy Wood's research on habit formation reveals that approximately 43% of our daily behaviors are habits—actions we perform automatically in response to consistent cues in our environment. These habits don't require decision-making or motivation; they happen because they're deeply embedded in our routines. Building on this, behavioral scientist BJ Fogg developed the concept of "habit stacking"—the practice of linking a new behavior to an existing habit. The formula is simple: After I [existing habit], I will [new ritual].

Studies show that people who use habit stacking are significantly more likely to maintain new behaviors long-term because they're leveraging existing neural pathways rather than trying to forge entirely new ones. The existing habit acts as a natural reminder and provides built-in structure.

Why This Works Better Than Motivation

Motivation fluctuates. It surges and fades. Existing habits, by contrast, are consistent. They happen pretty much automatically—which makes them the perfect anchor for new behaviors. When you stack a new ritual onto an existing habit, you're creating a sequence your brain already knows how to follow. The existing habit becomes the prompt, and over time, the new behavior becomes just as automatic.

Examples of Habit Stacking:

- *After I pour my morning coffee, I will write three things I'm grateful for.*
- *After I brush my teeth at night, I will lay out my workout clothes for tomorrow.*
- *After I close my laptop at the end of the workday, I will go for a 10-minute walk.*

The key is specificity. The more concrete your existing habit, the stronger the connection.

THIS WEEK'S FOCUS

→ **Identify your existing habits.** *What do you already do consistently: making coffee, brushing teeth, eating lunch, commuting, walking the dog. These are your anchors.*
→ **Stack your new rituals.** *For each weekly ritual you defined in your pre-work, attach it to an existing habit using the formula: "After I [existing habit], I will [new ritual]."*
→ **Make it visible.** *Write your habit stack somewhere you'll see it daily—a stick-note on your bathroom mirror or your fridge, a reminder in your phone. Visibility reinforces connection.*
→ **Start immediately.** *Don't wait for the perfect moment or the surge of motivation. Your existing habits are already happening. Let them carry your new rituals forward.*

The goal this week isn't perfection. It's integration. You're not building something from nothing—you're building on what already works.

PROGRESS TRACKER

GOAL # 1
RITUALS:
....
Scheduled for:
....
Accomplished:
....

GOAL # 2
RITUALS:
....
Scheduled for:
....
Accomplished:
....

GOAL # 3
RITUALS:
....
Scheduled for:
....
Accomplished:
....

THIS WEEK'S INSIGHTS AND LEARNINGS

What did this week teach me?
....

What's one achievement I'm proud of?
....

What's one thing I'll adjust next week?
....

WEEK 2: THE TWO-MINUTE RULE
START SMALLER THAN YOU THINK

You've made it through Week 1. You showed up for your rituals. Now comes the test: Can you keep going when the novelty wears off? The secret isn't willpower. It's making your rituals so small that skipping them feels harder than doing them.

The Research: The Habit Formular

Dr. BJ Fogg, a behavior scientist at Stanford, spent 20 years studying how habits form. His research revealed something counterintuitive: the best way to build a lasting habit isn't to go big—it's to go tiny. Fogg's formula:

$$Behavior = Motivation \times Ability \times Prompt$$

When motivation is high (like Week 1), you can do hard things. But motivation fluctuates. The only reliable way to maintain behavior is to make it ridiculously easy.

The Two-Minute Rule

Your ritual should take two minutes or less to complete. Not as a warm-up before the "real" thing. Two minutes total.

Examples:

- *Don't commit to "working out for 30 minutes."*
  *→ **Commit to laying out your workout clothes and putting the gym bag in the car.***
- *Don't commit to "writing 1,000 words."*
  *→ **Commit to opening your document and writing one sentence.***

Why? Because starting is the hardest part. Once you've started, momentum often takes over. But if the entry point feels too big, you'll never begin.

THIS WEEK'S FOCUS

→ Look at your rituals. Are any of them too ambitious? If you've been struggling to show up, shrink them. Make them so small that not doing them feels almost silly. That's when you know you've got it right.

→ The goal isn't to stay small forever. It's to build consistency.

PROGRESS TRACKER

GOAL # 1
RITUALS:

....

Scheduled for:

....

Accomplished:

....

GOAL # 2
RITUALS:

....

Scheduled for:

....

Accomplished:

....

GOAL # 3
RITUALS:

....

Scheduled for:

....

Accomplished:

....

THIS WEEK'S INSIGHTS AND LEARNINGS

What did this week teach me?

....

What's one achievement I'm proud of?

....

What's one thing I'll adjust next week?

....

WEEK 3: BUSTING THE MOTIVATION MYTH
ACTION CREATES MOTIVATION (NOT THE OTHER WAY AROUND)

Most people wait to feel motivated before they act. That's why most people quit. Here's what research shows: Motivation doesn't create action. Action creates motivation. The sequence is backward from what we expect.

The Research: The Progress Principle

Harvard professor Teresa Amabile studied thousands of workers to understand what drives motivation. Her finding? The single biggest motivator isn't rewards, recognition, or inspiration—**it's progress.**

Even small wins trigger a dopamine response in your brain. That hit of dopamine makes you want to keep going. But you can't feel progress until you've taken action first.

This is why waiting for motivation keeps you stuck. You're waiting for a feeling that can only come after you've already started.

The Action-Motivation Loop

So, what does that look like in real life? Here's how it actually works:

1. *You take action (even when you don't feel like it)*

2. *You experience a small win*

3. *Your brain releases dopamine*

4. *You feel motivated to continue*

5. *You take more action*

That's not a flaw in your willpower. That's how your brain is designed to work. The loop feeds itself—but only if you start it.

THIS WEEK'S FOCUS

→ **Notice the moments when you don't feel motivated. Instead of judging yourself, get curious. What happens if you act anyway?**

→ **Start your ritual. Do just five minutes. Then check in with yourself. Chances are, the motivation shows up halfway through. Not before. After.**

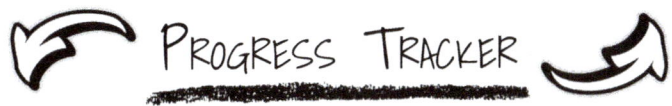

PROGRESS TRACKER

GOAL # 1
RITUALS:
....
Scheduled for:
....
Accomplished:
....

GOAL # 2
RITUALS:
....
Scheduled for:
....
Accomplished:
....

GOAL # 3
RITUALS:
....
Scheduled for:
....
Accomplished:
....

THIS WEEK'S INSIGHTS AND LEARNINGS

What did this week teach me?
....

What's one achievement I'm proud of?
....

What's one thing I'll adjust next week?
....

WEEK 4: CELEBRATING SMALL WINS
WHY RECOGNITION MATTERS MORE THAN RESULTS

Welcome to your new week! You've shown up consistently. That deserves recognition. But here's what most people do: they dismiss their progress. "It's only been three weeks." "I haven't seen results yet." "Anyone could do this." That dismissal is dangerous because your brain needs evidence that what you're doing is working—even when the outcomes aren't visible yet.

The Research: The Power of Celebration

In BJ Fogg's research on behavior change, celebration emerged as one of the most critical—and most overlooked—components of habit formation. When you celebrate immediately after completing a behavior, your brain releases dopamine. Dopamine acts as a reward signal, reinforcing the neural pathway associated with that behavior. Over time, your brain learns: "This behavior feels good. Let's do it again." Without celebration, even consistent behaviors can feel like drudgery. With celebration, they start to feel intrinsically rewarding.

What Celebration Looks Like

It doesn't need to be big. It just needs to be immediate and genuine.

Examples:

- *Checking off a box on your tracker with intention.*
- *A fist pump after finishing your ritual - or even a pat on your own shoulder.*
- *Saying "Yes!" out loud (I know... *awkward* — just give it a try. Your brain will love it!)*

Pick any celebratory movement or mental note that feels true to you. Practice it right now, so you know what to do next time you complete your task.

The key is timing. Celebrate within seconds of completing the behavior—not later, not when results show up. Right away.

THIS WEEK'S FOCUS

→ **After every ritual you complete, pause for two seconds. Acknowledge what you just did. Feel proud of it.**

→ **Get familiar with the mindset shift: You're not celebrating the outcome. You're celebrating the choice. Showing up. Keeping your word to yourself.**
That's what builds lasting change.

PROGRESS TRACKER

GOAL # 1
RITUALS:
....
Scheduled for:
....
Accomplished:
....

GOAL # 2
RITUALS:
....
Scheduled for:
....
Accomplished:
....

GOAL # 3
RITUALS:
....
Scheduled for:
....
Accomplished:
....

THIS WEEK'S INSIGHTS AND LEARNINGS

What did this week teach me?
....

What's one achievement I'm proud of?
....

What's one thing I'll adjust next week?
....

WEEK 5: ENVIRONMENTAL DESIGN
YOUR SURROUNDINGS SHAPE YOUR BEHAVIOR

You've been showing up for a few weeks now. But we all know how it is: some days feel harder than others. Often, the difference isn't willpower. It's your environment.

The Research: Friction and Flow

James Clear, author of Atomic Habits, synthesized decades of behavioral research into one principle: make good habits easy and bad habits hard.

The idea comes from studies on "choice architecture"—how the design of our environment influences our decisions without us realizing it.

Research shows that reducing friction by just one step can dramatically increase follow-through. And adding friction by just one step can dramatically decrease unwanted behaviors.

Examples of Environmental Design

To support good habits:

- *Put your workout clothes next to your bed (removes 1 step)*
- *Keep your journal on your pillow (visual cue)*
- *Prep your study materials the night before (eliminates morning decisions)*
- *Have fresh fruit sitting out visible (for convenience)*

To discourage bad habits:

- *Charge your phone outside your bedroom (adds friction to scrolling)*
- *Move social media apps to a folder away from your home screen*
- *Set screen-time limits - and don't extend them! (like, really: don't!)*
- *Put sweets and other unhealthy treats out of sight and harder to access*

THIS WEEK'S FOCUS

→ Look at your rituals and assess what one small change you can make to your environment that would make them easier?

→ Rearrange one space. Remove one obstacle. Add one visual cue.
Your environment should work for you, not against you.

PROGRESS TRACKER

GOAL # 1
RITUALS:

....

Scheduled for:

....

Accomplished:

....

GOAL # 2
RITUALS:

....

Scheduled for:

....

Accomplished:

....

GOAL # 3
RITUALS:

....

Scheduled for:

....

Accomplished:

....

THIS WEEK'S INSIGHTS AND LEARNINGS

What did this week teach me?

....

What's one achievement I'm proud of?

....

What's one thing I'll adjust next week?

....

WEEK 6: THE FIRST DIP
WHEN MOTIVATION FADES (AND WHAT TO DO ABOUT IT)

Welcome to the dip. This is where most people quit. Week 6 isn't glamorous. The novelty has worn off. The initial excitement is gone. Your rituals feel routine—maybe even boring. This is normal. And this is exactly where transformation happens.

The Research: The Enthusiasm Curve

Research on behavior change consistently shows a predictable pattern: enthusiasm peaks in Week 1-2, dips around Week 3-6, then gradually stabilizes around Week 8-12.

Psychologist Roy Baumeister calls this the "transition from motivation to habit." In the beginning, motivation carries you. But motivation is unreliable. The dip is when your brain starts building automaticity—the neural pathways that make behavior feel effortless. You're not losing momentum. You're building something deeper.

What the Dip Teaches You

The dip reveals whether your rituals are sustainable. If something feels unbearable at Week 6, it won't last to Week 52.

But if you can show up during the dip—even imperfectly—you're proving to yourself that this isn't about feeling inspired. It's about becoming someone new.

Examples:

- *Gym 4 days a week feels too much?*
  → Swap one or two days for a quick home workout or a brisk walk in your area.
- *Cooking wholesome meals every night is too time-consuming?*
  → Find a delicious-looking meal prep recipe online and add the ingredients to your shopping list.

The dip doesn't ask for perfection. It asks for presence.

THIS WEEK'S FOCUS

→ **Lower your expectations. Don't try to be perfect. Just show up.**

→ **Do the absolute minimum version of your ritual. Two minutes. One rep.**

→ **The goal isn't performance. It's presence. You're training your brain to trust that you'll keep going—even when nothing feels exciting. This is where real change begins.**

PROGRESS TRACKER

GOAL # 1
RITUALS:
....

Scheduled for:
....

Accomplished:
....

GOAL # 2
RITUALS:
....

Scheduled for:
....

Accomplished:
....

GOAL # 3
RITUALS:
....

Scheduled for:
....

Accomplished:
....

THIS WEEK'S INSIGHTS AND LEARNINGS

What did this week teach me?
....

What's one achievement I'm proud of?
....

What's one thing I'll adjust next week?
....

WEEK 7: IDENTITY OVER OUTCOMES
WHO ARE YOU BECOMING?

Seven weeks in, it's easy to focus on what you haven't achieved yet. You haven't lost the weight. You haven't finished the project. You haven't reached the milestone. But outcomes are lagging indicators. They show up long after the work has been done. Identity is a leading indicator. It shows up the moment you act.

The Research: Identity-Based Habits

James Clear's research distinguishes between **two types of goals:**

Outcome-based: *"I want to run a marathon."*

Identity-based: *"I am a runner."*

Studies show that people who frame their goals around identity are significantly more likely to sustain behavior long-term. Why? Because every action becomes a vote for the person you're becoming.

The Question That Changes Everything

Instead of asking, "What do I want to achieve?" ask: "Who do I want to become?" Every ritual you've completed over the past weeks is evidence of that new identity taking shape. Each time you show up for your ritual—no matter how small—you're casting a vote: "I am someone who does this." Over time, those votes add up. Your self-concept shifts. And once your identity changes, the behaviors follow naturally.

THIS WEEK'S FOCUS

→ **Reframe your rituals as identity statements.**

Instead of: "I'm going to the gym today."
Try: "I'm someone who prioritizes movement."

Instead of: "I need to study."
Try: "I'm someone who invests in growth."

→ **Notice how that small shift changes how the ritual feels. You're not checking off a task. You're becoming someone new.**

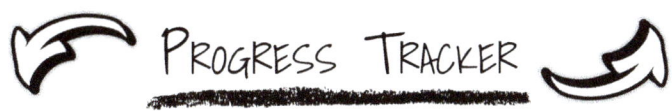

PROGRESS TRACKER

GOAL # 1
RITUALS:
....
Scheduled for:
....
Accomplished:
....

GOAL # 2
RITUALS:
....
Scheduled for:
....
Accomplished:
....

GOAL # 3
RITUALS:
....
Scheduled for:
....
Accomplished:
....

THIS WEEK'S INSIGHTS AND LEARNINGS

What did this week teach me?
....

What's one achievement I'm proud of?
....

What's one thing I'll adjust next week?
....

WEEK 8: PROGRESS OVER PERFECTION
GOOD ENOUGH IS BETTER THAN NOTHING

Eight weeks ago, you set ambitious goals. You defined quarterly milestones. You committed to weekly rituals. And chances are, it hasn't gone all perfectly. You've missed days. You've scaled back. You've adjusted. That's not failure. That's learning.

The Research: The "Good Enough" Principle

Research in behavioral psychology shows that perfectionism is one of the biggest barriers to sustained change. Perfectionists are more likely to quit after a single setback because they interpret imperfection as failure. But studies on habit formation reveal the opposite: consistency beats intensity every time. Missing one day doesn't derail progress. Missing two days in a row starts to threaten the habit. The key is the "never miss twice" rule—coined by habit researcher BJ Fogg.
One miss is life. Two misses are the beginning of a new pattern.

What "Good Enough" Looks Like

Some days, your ritual will be excellent. You'll feel strong, focused, and energized. On other days, your ritual will be minimal. You'll do two minutes and call it done. Both days count. Both days are wins.

The excellent days build momentum. The minimal days build trust—trust that you'll show up even when it's hard, even when nothing feels perfect.

THIS WEEK'S FOCUS

→ If you've been aiming for perfection, release it. Aim for consistency instead.

→ Did you show up? Even for two minutes? That's enough.

→ Continue tracking your effort, not just your outcomes. Give yourself credit for showing up on the hard days—those are your proof that you can do it!

→ Remember: Progress isn't linear. Keep going and trust the process.

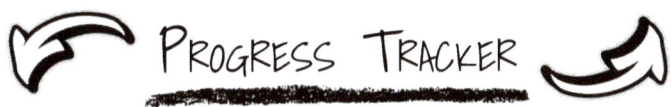

PROGRESS TRACKER

GOAL # 1
RITUALS:
....
Scheduled for:
....
Accomplished:
....

GOAL # 2
RITUALS:
....
Scheduled for:
....
Accomplished:
....

GOAL # 3
RITUALS:
....
Scheduled for:
....
Accomplished:
....

THIS WEEK'S INSIGHTS AND LEARNINGS

What did this week teach me?
....

What's one achievement I'm proud of?
....

What's one thing I'll adjust next week?
....

Week 9: When You Skip a Day (or a Week)
Missing Once Isn't Failure

Let's address what might have already happened: you missed a ritual. Maybe more than one. You told yourself you'd show up every day. And then life happened. You got sick. Work exploded. You simply forgot. Now you're wondering if you've ruined everything? You haven't. Just pick up exactly where you left off.

The Research: The "What-the-Hell Effect"

Studies show that attempting to compensate makes people actually less likely to return. Psychologist Janet Polivy's research on the "What-the-Hell Effect" reveals this dangerous pattern: when people break a commitment, they respond by either giving up entirely or trying to "make up for it" with excessive effort. Both responses increase the likelihood of quitting.

When you miss a workout and tell yourself, "I'll do double tomorrow," you've raised the barrier to starting again. The compensation creates pressure. And pressure creates avoidance.

The good news? Research on habit resilience shows that people who return immediately at normal intensity are just as likely to maintain long-term change as those who never miss.

The Compassionate Return

The key is to treat each miss as isolated—not as evidence that you're "bad at this" or that the habit is failing. One missed day doesn't erase weeks of showing up. When you miss, your self-talk matters. Shame keeps you stuck. Curiosity moves you forward.

Instead of: "I'm so lazy. I always quit. I knew this wasn't going to work."
Try: "I missed yesterday. What got in the way? How can I make it easier to return today?"

The first response reinforces an old identity. The second opens the door to learning and growth. Compassion isn't letting yourself off the hook. It's choosing a response that makes returning possible instead of impossible.

This Week's Focus

→ **If you've missed recently, return today.**

→ **No guilt. No "making up for it". Just do your ritual once, at normal intensity.**

→ **One action erases the miss. That's all it takes.**

PROGRESS TRACKER

GOAL # 1
RITUALS:
....

Scheduled for:
....
Accomplished:
....

GOAL # 2
RITUALS:
....

Scheduled for:
....
Accomplished:
....

GOAL # 3
RITUALS:
....

Scheduled for:
....
Accomplished:
....

THIS WEEK'S INSIGHTS AND LEARNINGS

What did this week teach me?

....

What's one achievement I'm proud of?

....

What's one thing I'll adjust next week?

....

WEEK 10: THE STORIES YOU TELL YOURSELF
YOUR INTERNAL NARRATIVE SHAPES YOUR REALITY

By Week 10, you've gathered evidence. You've shown up. You've missed. You've adjusted. You've kept going. So, let's take a look at the story you're telling yourself about it all.

The Research: Self-Concept and Behavior

Psychologist Carol Dweck's research on mindset reveals something powerful: the stories we tell ourselves about who we are directly influence what we're capable of becoming. People with a "fixed mindset" believe their abilities are static and unchangeable. People with a "growth mindset" believe abilities can be developed through effort and learning.

The difference isn't just semantic—it's neurological. Your brain treats these narratives as predictions and works to prove them true. When you repeatedly tell yourself "I'm not disciplined," your brain looks for evidence to confirm that belief. When you say "I'm building discipline," your brain seeks proof of growth. Studies in neuroplasticity support this: our self-concept literally shapes which neural pathways strengthen and which weaken over time.

Common Limiting Beliefs (And How to Reframe Them)

Fixed mindset statements close off possibilities. They become self-fulfilling prophecies. Therefore, all you need to do is reframe negative assumptions into intention statements.

Examples:

- *"I'm not a morning person."* → **"I'm learning to wake up earlier."**
- *"I'm bad at staying consistent."* → **"I'm building consistency."**
- *"I always quit things."* → **"I'm someone who keeps trying."**
- *"I'm not disciplined enough."* → **"I'm developing discipline through practice."**
- *"I don't have enough time."* → **"I'm learning to prioritize what matters."**
- *"Other people can do this, but I can't."* → **"I'm capable of learning new skills."**

THIS WEEK'S FOCUS

→ **Write down one limiting belief you've noticed yourself repeating:**

....

→ **Then rewrite it as a growth statement.**

....

→ **Notice how the reframe opens space for change. You're not fixed. You're becoming.**

PROGRESS TRACKER

GOAL # 1
RITUALS:

....

Scheduled for:

....

Accomplished:

....

GOAL # 2
RITUALS:

....

Scheduled for:

....

Accomplished:

....

GOAL # 3
RITUALS:

....

Scheduled for:

....

Accomplished:

....

THIS WEEK'S INSIGHTS AND LEARNINGS

What did this week teach me?

....

What's one achievement I'm proud of?

....

What's one thing I'll adjust next week?

....

Week 11: Accountability Without Shame
Finding Support That Actually Helps

You're almost through Season One. You've built momentum. You've navigated the dip. You've returned after missing. But here's a question: does anyone else know you're doing this?

The Research: Social Accountability

Studies on behavior change consistently show that accountability increases follow-through. But not all accountability is created equal.

Research by psychologist Ayelet Fishbach distinguishes between two types:

Outcome accountability: Someone checks if you achieved the result.
→ Did you lose weight? Did you finish the project?)
Process accountability: Someone checks if you showed up for the behavior.
→ Did you go to the gym? Did you write today?

Process accountability is far more effective for habit formation because it focuses on what you can control: your actions, not your outcomes.

Who Makes a Good Accountability Partner

Not someone who judges or shames you.
Not someone who needs updates on your "progress."

Someone who simply asks: "Did you do your ritual today?"
And responds with: "Great. Talk to you next week."

The best accountability is neutral, consistent, and focused on showing up - not performing.

You don't need coaching or cheerleading. You just need a gentle witness—someone who knows you're committed and reminds you that you're not doing this alone.

This Week's Focus

→ **Choose someone who won't judge or pressure you. Tell them about your rituals.**

→ **Ask them to check in once a week, like: "Did you do your rituals this week?"**

→ **Decide how you'll touch base. Text every Sunday? Monthly coffee? Quick voice note? Choose what feels natural and *actually* doable to you.**

PROGRESS TRACKER

GOAL # 1
RITUALS:
....
Scheduled for:
....
Accomplished:
....

GOAL # 2
RITUALS:
....
Scheduled for:
....
Accomplished:
....

GOAL # 3
RITUALS:
....
Scheduled for:
....
Accomplished:
....

THIS WEEK'S INSIGHTS AND LEARNINGS

What did this week teach me?
....

What's one achievement I'm proud of?
....

What's one thing I'll adjust next week?
....

WEEK 12: YOU'VE BUILT SOMETHING REAL
CELEBRATING CONSISTENCY

Twelve weeks ago, you planted a seed. You defined your goals. You built your rituals. Since then, you showed up—again and again, even when it was hard. Well done! Seriously. That's amazing!

The Research: The Power of Small Wins

Research by psychologist Karl Weick on "small wins theory" shows that consistent, incremental progress creates a powerful psychological effect: it builds momentum, increases confidence, and strengthens belief in future success.

Studies on self-efficacy by Albert Bandura reveal that "mastery experiences"—proving to yourself that you can do something—are the most powerful source of confidence. Each time you complete a ritual, you're not just building a habit. You're building evidence that you're someone who follows through.

Even neuroscience research supports this: repetition over time strengthens neural pathways, making behaviors feel more automatic and requiring less conscious effort.

After 12 weeks of consistency, your brain has literally rewired itself to support your new rituals.

What 12 Weeks of Showing Up Creates

You've gathered proof that you're capable of sustained change. Even if progress feels subtle, you've built three critical things:

- **Momentum:** *You've shown up enough times that continuing feels easier than stopping*
- **Identity shift:** *You're no longer "trying to be" someone. You're someone who does it.*
- **Trust:** *You've proven to yourself that you'll keep your word, even when motivation fades.*

THIS WEEK'S FOCUS

→ **Acknowledge one ritual that feels easier now than it did in Week 1.**

→ **Notice how it's become part of your routine. That's automaticity building.**

→ **Celebrate your completion rate—not perfection.**
Did you show up for 80% of your rituals? Or just about 2 out of 3 times?
Even just 50% is better than the zero you started with.
Keep that in mind!

PROGRESS TRACKER

GOAL # 1
RITUALS:
....

Scheduled for:
....
Accomplished:
....

GOAL # 2
RITUALS:
....

Scheduled for:
....
Accomplished:
....

GOAL # 3
RITUALS:
....

Scheduled for:
....
Accomplished:
....

THIS WEEK'S INSIGHTS AND LEARNINGS

What did this week teach me?
....

What's one achievement I'm proud of?
....

What's one thing I'll adjust next week?
....

25% MILESTONE REFLECTION
You've Made It Further Than Most

Let's talk about what you've accomplished.

As we all know, most New Year's resolutions fail within the first month. A study by the University of Scranton found that by Week 12, only 8% of people are still working toward their goals — which is why you decided to go along with this fantastic book and finally break that pattern. And you did it! Well done: **You're officially in the 8%**.

You didn't just rely on motivation and good intentions.

- *You built a system.*
- *You defined goals, broke them into milestones, and created weekly rituals.*
- *You showed up after the initial excitement and conquered the motivation dip.*
- *You faced the reality of life getting in the way, and still found the time to continue.*

That's not luck. That's structure. That's resilience. That's growth.

Why Your Approach Works

Psychologist John Norcross studied resolution success rates for over two decades. His findings reveal three critical factors that determine who maintains change and who abandons it:

- **Specificity:** Vague goals fail at dramatically higher rates than specific, measurable behaviors. You didn't just set vague goals—you defined exactly what your rituals look like and when they happen.

- **Self-monitoring:** People who track their behavior are significantly more likely to maintain habits long-term. You've been tracking your progress for twelve weeks.

- **Adaptive mindset:** You've learned to return after missing. You've reframed setbacks as data, not failure.

Most people set goals without understanding the science of behavior change. They expect willpower to carry them through. They don't plan for the motivation dip. They don't design their environment. They don't celebrate small wins.

You've done all of that. And that's why you're still here. And you're going on!

This Week's Focus:

Your Season One – Looking Back and Ahead

Before you move into the next season, use this week to assess where you are. Not to judge—but to gain clarity for the next stretch of the journey.

Complete the following 5 steps. You can do one each day to stay consistent while keeping it light, split them over 2 or 3 days, or answer them all in one sitting—whatever works best with your rhythm and feels doable.

Step 1: Review Your Goals and Milestones

Go back to the *goals* you set in the introduction. For each one, ask yourself:

- *Does this goal still feel aligned with who I want to become?*
- *Has anything shifted that requires adjustment?*

It's okay if your goals have evolved. You're not locked in.

....

Goal #1

....

Goal #2

....

Goal #3

....

Now look at your *milestones* for each.

- *Did you achieve them?*
- *Exceed them?*
- *Fall short?*

All outcomes provide valuable learning. If you exceeded expectations, consider setting a higher target for the next season. If you fell short, ask yourself why—and whether your next milestone needs to be more realistic.

....

Goal #1: 25% Milestone ☐ *achieved*   ☐ *exceeded*   ☐ *fell short*

My 50% Milestone will be:

....

Goal #2: 25% Milestone ☐ *achieved*   ☐ *exceeded*   ☐ *fell short*

My 50% Milestone will be:

....

Goal #3: 25% Milestone ☐ *achieved*   ☐ *exceeded*   ☐ *fell short*

My 50% Milestone will be:

....

Step 2: Identify Your Patterns

You've gathered twelve weeks of data about yourself. Awareness is the first step to change. When you acknowledge your patterns, you can align your rhythm with them.

....

When do you show up most consistently?
Time of day, day of week, circumstances?

....

When do you struggle most?
What triggers make it harder?

....

What helps you return after missing?
What Mindset, strategy, or support gets you back on track?

....

Step 3: Develop Your Next Rituals

For your Sprout Season's milestones, design rituals that leverage what you've learned about yourself. Make them specific, and make them sustainable.

....

Goal #1: 50% Milestone

....

Weekly Rituals   →

        →

        →

....
....

Goal #2: 50% Milestone

....

Weekly Rituals   →

        →

        →

....
....

Goal #3: 50% Milestone

....

Weekly Rituals   →

        →

        →

....

Step 4: Acknowledge Your Wins

Write at least three things you're genuinely proud of from the past 12 weeks. These don't need to be dramatic. "I showed up even when I didn't feel like it" is a massive win. "I returned the day after missing" counts. "I didn't judge myself when I struggled" is growth. Name your victories—no matter how small they feel.

....

....

....

....

Step 5: Set One Intention for the Next Season

Your upcoming Sprout Season is about nurturing small habits through the messy middle. Progress will feel slower. Doubt may creep in. But you'll also start to see something powerful: your rituals becoming automatic. What's one thing you want to focus on in the next 12 weeks?

Examples:

- *"I want to return faster after missing."*
- *"I want to stop judging my progress so harshly."*
- *"I want to trust the process even when I can't see results."*

....

My intention for the next season:

....

....

A Note Before Moving Forward

The upcoming Sprout Season might not feel as thrilling as the first. The novelty has faded. Your rituals may feel repetitive. Some days, you might even question whether any of this is working. That's normal.
Remember: You've already done the hard work of starting. You've planted your intentions, built a structure, and continued to show up.
Now, it's time to nurture what you've started. Progress may be quieter here, but it's no less powerful. Keep going — especially now. This will be where transformation becomes real.

WEEK 14: TRUST THE PROCESS
THE BREAKTHROUGH IS BUILDING

Welcome to the second part of your One Year from Yesterday. How are you feeling today?

If you're feeling less excited than in Week 1, congratulations. You've entered the most important phase of growth—the one most people never reach because they quit too early. The messy middle isn't a sign that something's wrong. It's a sign you're doing it right.

The Research: The Plateau of Latent Potential

James Clear describes a phenomenon he calls "the plateau of latent potential"—the gap between when you start working and when you start seeing results. Imagine an ice cube on a table in a slowly warming room. At 25 degrees Fahrenheit, nothing happens. At 28 degrees, still frozen. At 31 degrees—no visible change. Then, at 32 degrees, the ice melts. All the heat you brought on, at 25, 28, and 31 - all the work you put in to get here, it mattered. The change was happening—it just wasn't visible yet.

This is where you are now. You're doing the work. Neural pathways are forming. Habits are taking root. The evidence just hasn't crossed the visibility threshold.

Here's the empowering truth: recognizing you're in a plateau means you're already ahead. Most people quit here because they don't understand what's happening. But you do. And that awareness changes everything.

When Routine Becomes Your Advantage

When rituals start to feel automatic, your brain is doing exactly what it's supposed to do: conserving energy by moving behavior from conscious effort to unconscious routine. What feels mundane is actually mastery emerging. The fact that something no longer requires intense focus means it's integrating into who you are.

THIS WEEK'S FOCUS

→ **Reframe "boring" as "working." Automaticity is the goal.**
If your ritual feels routine, that's not a problem—that's progress.

→ **Celebrate the plateau. You're in the threshold zone. The breakthrough is coming, but only if you stay.**

→ **Show up without needing proof. Trust the process even when results aren't visible. The heat is rising. The ice is warming. Keep going.**

PROGRESS TRACKER

GOAL # 1
RITUALS:

Scheduled for:

Accomplished:

GOAL # 2
RITUALS:

Scheduled for:

Accomplished:

GOAL # 3
RITUALS:

Scheduled for:

Accomplished:

THIS WEEK'S INSIGHTS AND LEARNINGS

What did this week teach me?

What's one achievement I'm proud of?

What's one thing I'll adjust next week?

Week 15: Your Driving Force
Connecting to Your Deeper "Why"

You've built a structure. You've proven you can be consistent. But here's the uncomfortable truth: structure alone isn't enough. If it were, everyone with a good plan would succeed. The difference between goals that stick and goals that fade isn't willpower. It's meaning.

This week is about excavating your "why." Not the surface-level reason you tell yourself. The real one. The one that makes you feel something when you say it out loud.

The Research: Intrinsic Motivation and Long-Term Change

Psychologist Edward Deci's research on self-determination theory reveals a crucial distinction in motivation: external vs. internal.

External motivation comes from outside rewards—approval, recognition, appearance, status. It can get you started, but it fades quickly. Once the reward is achieved (or feels unattainable), motivation disappears.

Internal motivation comes from alignment—the feeling that what you're doing is true to who you are and who you want to become. It doesn't depend on anyone else noticing.

It doesn't need applause. It sustains itself because it feels right, even when it's hard. Studies consistently show that people driven by intrinsic motivation maintain behavior change significantly longer than those driven by external rewards. Why? Because internal alignment creates devotion, not dependency.

The Motivation Hierarchy

Here's how motivation typically evolves:

- *Level 1: External validation — "I want others to see me as successful."*
- *Level 2: Outcome achievement — "I want to reach this specific result."*
- *Level 3: Internal alignment — "I want to feel like I'm living in integrity with my values."*

The deeper you go, the more sustainable your motivation becomes. Let's say your goal is to "be healthier." Okay—but why?

- *So you have more energy? Why does that matter?*
- *So you feel confident? Why does that matter?*
- *So you can keep up with your kids? Why does that matter?*
- *So you feel alive in your body instead of disconnected from it?*

Now we're getting somewhere. The first answer is rarely the real answer. Keep asking "why" until you feel something shift in your chest. That's when you've hit the truth.

This Week's Focus

→ **Take your intention and ask "why?" five times.**
Write each answer down. Let yourself go deeper with each question.
→ **Identify whether your motivation is primarily external or internal.**
Be honest. If it's external right now, that's okay—just know that you'll need to find the internal connection to sustain this long-term. So, ask why this matters one more time!
→ **Write your deepest "why" somewhere visible. This becomes your anchor.**

PROGRESS TRACKER

GOAL # 1
RITUALS:

....

Scheduled for:

....

Accomplished:

....

GOAL # 2
RITUALS:

....

Scheduled for:

....

Accomplished:

....

GOAL # 3
RITUALS:

....

Scheduled for:

....

Accomplished:

....

THIS WEEK'S INSIGHTS AND LEARNINGS

What did this week teach me?

....

What's one achievement I'm proud of?

....

What's one thing I'll adjust next week?

....

WEEK 16: THE COMPARISON TRAP
YOUR ONLY COMPETITION IS YESTERDAY'S VERSION OF YOU

You're cruising along on this journey. And if you're anything like most people, you've probably started noticing what others are doing. Maybe someone you know seems further along. Maybe they're sharing their wins online. Maybe their progress looks effortless.

Here's what's important to remember: looking to others for inspiration is healthy. Seeing what's possible can motivate you. Learning from their strategies can help you grow.

But comparing your progress to theirs? That's where things get dangerous. Their life, their circumstances, their starting point—none of it matches yours. Measuring yourself against their journey will only drain the energy you need for your own.

The Research: Social Comparison and Motivation

Psychologist Leon Festinger's social comparison theory explains why we're wired to compare ourselves to others—it's how we evaluate our own abilities and progress. But research also shows that upward social comparison (comparing yourself to people who seem "ahead" of you) can be highly demotivating. It triggers feelings of inadequacy, discouragement, and self-doubt.

Studies on motivation reveal that **the most sustainable form of comparison is self-comparison**: measuring your progress against where you were, not where someone else is.

The Highlight Reel Problem

Social media makes this worse. You see someone else's polished post and assume their journey has been effortless.

You don't see the days they missed. You don't see the earlier dips they went through. You don't see the adjustments they made when things didn't go as planned.

You're comparing your full story—with all its messy, imperfect reality—to someone else's highlight reel.

THIS WEEK'S FOCUS

→ **When you catch yourself comparing, redirect your attention. Ask yourself:**
   ✧ *Am I further along than I was in Week 1?*
   ✧ *Have I learned something about myself that I didn't know before?*
   ✧ *Am I still showing up, even imperfectly?*
If the answer is yes, you're winning. Even if it doesn't look like anyone else's version of winning.

→ **Take a look at your Social Media Feed:**
   ✧ Unfollow or mute accounts that make you feel "behind."
   ✧ Keep following only what motivates and inspires you.
Reconnect with your own pace.

PROGRESS TRACKER

GOAL # 1
RITUALS:
....
Scheduled for:
....
Accomplished:
....

GOAL # 2
RITUALS:
....
Scheduled for:
....
Accomplished:
....

GOAL # 3
RITUALS:
....
Scheduled for:
....
Accomplished:
....

THIS WEEK'S INSIGHTS AND LEARNINGS

What did this week teach me?

....

What's one achievement I'm proud of?

....

What's one thing I'll adjust next week?

....

WEEK 17: ENERGY MANAGEMENT OVER TIME MANAGEMENT
NOT ALL HOURS ARE CREATED EQUAL

You've been protecting time for your rituals. You've scheduled them. You've set alarms. You've shown up. But here's what most people don't talk about: often, time isn't the issue. Energy is. You can have an hour blocked on your calendar, but if your energy is depleted, that hour won't be productive.

The Research: Ultradian Rhythms and Peak Performance

Research on human performance reveals that our energy fluctuates throughout the day in 90-120 minute cycles called **ultradian rhythms**. During peak windows, your focus is sharp, your willpower is strong, and tasks feel manageable. During low windows, everything feels harder—even simple tasks require more effort.

Most people have 2-3 peak energy windows per day:
- Morning (often 8-11 am for many people)
- Mid-afternoon (sometimes 2-4 pm, though this varies)
- Evening (for some, a second wind around 7-9 pm)

Studies show that trying to "power through" low-energy windows depletes will-power faster and leads to burnout. The most effective approach? Work with your natural rhythm, not against it.

Identifying Your Peak Windows

In order to align your tasks with your natural energy levels, start by noticing your individual pattern. Look out for the following:

Signs you're in a peak window:
- Tasks feel manageable and clear
- You can focus without fighting distractions
- Decisions come easily
- You have both mental clarity and physical energy
- You feel in control

Signs you're in a low-energy window:
- Everything feels harder than it should
- You're easily distracted or irritable
- Simple tasks require significant willpower
- You're drawn to avoidance behaviors (social media, snacks, procrastination)
- You're overthinking and stagnating

THIS WEEK'S FOCUS

→ **Track your energy for three days. Note when you feel most focused and when you feel most drained.**

→ **Then, look at your rituals. Are you scheduling them during your peak windows—or during your lowest energy times?**

→ **If possible, move one ritual to align with your natural energy. You'll be surprised how much easier it becomes.**

PROGRESS TRACKER

GOAL # 1
RITUALS:

Scheduled for:

Accomplished:

GOAL # 2
RITUALS:

Scheduled for:

Accomplished:

GOAL # 3
RITUALS:

Scheduled for:

Accomplished:

THIS WEEK'S INSIGHTS AND LEARNINGS

What did this week teach me?

What's one achievement I'm proud of?

What's one thing I'll adjust next week?

WEEK 18: THE ROLE OF REST
RECOVERY IS PART OF THE PROCESS

Welcome to week 18. How are you feeling? Have you been experiencing fatigue or exhaustion recently? Maybe not just physically—but mentally and emotionally, too?

That is entirely normal - and part of every successful growth journey. You've been showing up consistently. You've pushed through the dip. You've navigated comparison and energy management.

And now, your body and brain are asking for something you might feel guilty about: rest.

The Research: The Science of Recovery

Neuroscientist Dr. Sara Mednick's research on rest and performance reveals something crucial: **rest is not the opposite of productivity. It's a requirement for it.**
When you rest, your brain doesn't shut down. It consolidates learning, processes experiences, and strengthens the neural pathways you've been building through your rituals.
Studies on habit formation show that sleep and downtime are when behaviors become automatic. The repetitions you do while awake plant the seeds, but rest is what allows them to take root.

Active Rest vs. Numbing

There's a difference between rest that restores you and activities that numb you.

- **Active rest includes**: *sleep, walks in nature, stretching, meditation, reading, a wellness treatment or spa day, quality time with loved ones—activities that replenish your energy.*
- **Numbing includes**: *endless scrolling, binge-watching without intention, staying perpetually busy to avoid stillness, drinking to disconnect, online shopping spirals—activities that drain you further while giving the illusion of rest.*

The good news? Once you recognize the difference, you can choose what your body and mind actually need.

THIS WEEK'S FOCUS

→ **Schedule one intentional rest day this week. Protect it like you protect your rituals.**

→ **On that day, do something that genuinely restores you. Notice how you feel afterward.**

→ **Rest isn't lazy. Rest is strategic. It's what sustains your progress in the long run.**

PROGRESS TRACKER

GOAL # 1
RITUALS:
....

Scheduled for:
....

Accomplished:
....

GOAL # 2
RITUALS:
....

Scheduled for:
....

Accomplished:
....

GOAL # 3
RITUALS:
....

Scheduled for:
....

Accomplished:
....

THIS WEEK'S INSIGHTS AND LEARNINGS

What did this week teach me?
....

What's one achievement I'm proud of?
....

What's one thing I'll adjust next week?
....

Week 19: When Progress Feels Invisible
Trusting the Underground Work

You've been showing up consistently for nearly five months now. You've built rituals. You've stayed committed through the dip. Nevertheless, some days might still feel off. You look in the mirror or check your progress, and the results just don't match the picture you had in your head. The gap between effort and evidence can feel discouraging. This is one of the hardest parts of any growth journey. And it's where continued trust in the process is essential.

The Research: The Bamboo Growth Pattern

Chinese bamboo has one of nature's most remarkable growth patterns. When planted, it shows no visible growth for four to five years (yes, years!) Or, in other words, for over 50 months, not a single shoot breaks through the soil. During this time, the bamboo is building an extensive root system underground—spreading, strengthening, preparing. Then, in the fifth year, the bamboo grows up to 90 feet in just six weeks. Some species can even reach daily growth rates of almost 3 feet a day! You can literally watch it grow!

Research on skill acquisition and behavior change mirrors this pattern. Psychologist K. Anders Ericsson's studies on expertise show that improvement often happens in bursts—long periods of practice with minimal visible progress, followed by sudden leaps.

Why Invisible Doesn't Mean Ineffective

You're still in the root-building phase. Growth is happening—even if you might not see it yet. Every time you show up for your ritual, you are:

- *Strengthening neural pathways that make the behavior more automatic*
- *Building trust with yourself that you're someone who follows through*
- *Creating a foundation for future growth that will feel effortless*

Your work isn't wasted. It's compounding. Small, consistent actions accumulate into substantial change—all you have to do is stay long enough to witness its power unfold.

This Week's Focus

→ **List five things you've done consistently, even if you can't "see" results yet.**

→ **Acknowledge one thing that's become easier since you started.**

→ **Continue doing these things regularly. Your job is to keep building the roots. Trust the process.**

PROGRESS TRACKER

GOAL # 1
RITUALS:
....
Scheduled for:
....
Accomplished:
....

GOAL # 2
RITUALS:
....
Scheduled for:
....
Accomplished:
....

GOAL # 3
RITUALS:
....
Scheduled for:
....
Accomplished:
....

THIS WEEK'S INSIGHTS AND LEARNINGS

What did this week teach me?

....

What's one achievement I'm proud of?

....

What's one thing I'll adjust next week?

....

WEEK 20: ADJUSTING WITHOUT ABANDONING
THE DIFFERENCE BETWEEN QUITTING AND PIVOTING

Twenty weeks in, you've gathered a lot of experience about what works and what doesn't. Some rituals feel natural now. Others still feel like a struggle. And that's okay.

But here's the question: when do you adjust your approach—and when do you stay the course?

The Research: Flexibility Within Structure

Research on goal attainment distinguishes between two types of persistence:

- **Rigid persistence**: Continuing the same approach even when it's clearly not working, out of stubbornness or fear of "giving up."
- **Flexible persistence**: Staying committed to the goal while adjusting the strategy based on what you're learning.

Studies show that flexible persistence leads to significantly higher success rates. The people who achieve long-term change aren't the ones who never adjust—they're the ones who stay committed to the outcome while remaining open to changing the path.

The Questions to Ask

If a ritual feels unsustainable or has become irrelevant, assess it by answering these reflections :

- *Is this goal still aligned with who I'm becoming?*
  - → *If no, let it go without guilt.*
- *Is the goal still right, but the ritual needs adjustment?*
  - → *If yes, modify the approach.*
- *Am I resisting because it's hard, or because it's wrong?*
  - → *Hard is worth pushing through. Wrong is worth releasing.*

Course-correcting isn't failure. It's actually pretty smart! Take it as a sign that you are evolving on your journey.

THIS WEEK'S FOCUS

→ **Review your rituals. If one feels like it's no longer serving you, give yourself permission to adjust.**

→ **Shrink it. Change the timing. Swap it for a different approach. Stay committed to the direction—but be flexible about the path.**

PROGRESS TRACKER

GOAL # 1
RITUALS:

....

Scheduled for:
....

Accomplished:
....

GOAL # 2
RITUALS:

....

Scheduled for:
....

Accomplished:
....

GOAL # 3
RITUALS:

....

Scheduled for:
....

Accomplished:
....

THIS WEEK'S INSIGHTS AND LEARNINGS

What did this week teach me?

....

What's one achievement I'm proud of?

....

What's one thing I'll adjust next week?

....

WEEK 21: THE COMPANY YOU KEEP
YOUR ENVIRONMENT INCLUDES PEOPLE

You've already learned how to design your physical environment to support your rituals —remember, back in Week 5? Now let's look at another layer of the environment that powerfully shapes your success: the people around you. The people you spend time with influence your behavior—often invisibly. Some relationships fuel your growth. Others drain your resolve. And as you continue to change, you'll need to be intentional about who gets access to your energy.

The Research: Social Contagion

Research by Dr. Nicholas Christakis and Dr. James Fowler on social networks reveals something startling: behaviors spread through social networks like contagion. If someone in your close network adopts a new habit, you're significantly more likely to adopt it too—even if you're not consciously trying to.

But the reverse is also true. If the people around you dismiss your goals, downplay your progress, or subtly undermine your efforts, it becomes exponentially harder to sustain change.

Studies show that having even one person who supports your growth increases your likelihood of maintaining behavior change by over 50%.

Energy Givers vs. Energy Takers

Some relationships fuel your growth. Others drain your resolve.

- **Energy givers:** *people who celebrate your wins, respect your boundaries, and support your becoming—even when it's different from who you were before.*
- **Energy takers**: *people who minimize your efforts, question your choices, or need you to stay the same because your growth makes them uncomfortable.*

Your growth flourishes when you're surrounded by people who celebrate who you're be-coming, not just who you've been.

THIS WEEK'S FOCUS

→ **Identify one person who genuinely supports your growth. Spend intentional time with them this week.**

→ **If you need to, set a boundary with someone whose energy depletes you. Protecting your growth isn't selfish. It's an act of self-respect.**

PROGRESS TRACKER

GOAL # 1
RITUALS:

Scheduled for:

Accomplished:

GOAL # 2
RITUALS:

Scheduled for:

Accomplished:

GOAL # 3
RITUALS:

Scheduled for:

Accomplished:

THIS WEEK'S INSIGHTS AND LEARNINGS

What did this week teach me?

....

What's one achievement I'm proud of?

....

What's one thing I'll adjust next week?

....

WEEK 22: CELEBRATING SMALL WINS
BUILDING YOUR VICTORY LIST

Do you recall when we talked about the energizing effects of celebration? Back in Week 4, you learned that dopamine reinforces behavior and that rewarding yourself immediately after completing a ritual helps your brain want to repeat it. But here's what often happens as you move along on your growth journey: the rituals feel routine. The wins feel small. You stop acknowledging them.

That's exactly when momentum starts to fade. So, let's get that dopamine pumping again. This week is about remembering what you already know: small wins deserve recognition—not only at the beginning! Celebrating small wins continues to matter even more as time goes on, because it sustains your motivation when dramatic progress isn't visible just yet.

The Research: The Progress Principle

Harvard professor Teresa Amabile's research revealed something counterintuitive about long-term motivation: **the importance of acknowledging progress doesn't diminish as you get better—it intensifies**. In her studies, people who had been working on projects for months were more vulnerable to motivational collapse than beginners. Why? Because as behaviors become routine, the brain stops registering them as achievements. What once felt like a victory now feels like "just what I do." Without conscious celebration, your brain interprets consistency as unremarkable. But, it doesn't have to be that way: when people deliberately acknowledged their small wins—even after weeks or months of repetition—they maintained significantly higher engagement and resilience. The act of celebration signals to your brain that this still matters, preventing the psychological drift that causes people to abandon long-term goals.

Creating a Victory List

A victory list is a simple practice: at the end of each week, you write down 3-5 small wins. Not outcomes. Not achievements. Just evidence that you showed up.

Examples:

- *"I did my ritual even though I was exhausted."*
- *"I returned the day after missing."*
- *"I didn't judge myself when I struggled."*

You're making progress every single week. But if you're not acknowledging it, your brain doesn't register it as meaningful.

THIS WEEK'S FOCUS

→ Start your victory list. At the end of each day this week, name one small win out loud. Do a rewarding gesture or movement. Laugh, jump, clap.
Still feels silly? Do it anyway - it's scientifically proven. What's the worst that can happen?

→ You're training your brain to notice progress, even when it feels ordinary.

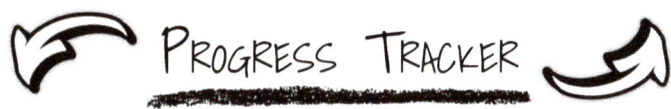

PROGRESS TRACKER

GOAL # 1
RITUALS:

Scheduled for:

Accomplished:

GOAL # 2
RITUALS:

Scheduled for:

Accomplished:

GOAL # 3
RITUALS:

Scheduled for:

Accomplished:

THIS WEEK'S INSIGHTS AND LEARNINGS

What did this week teach me?

What's one achievement I'm proud of?

What's one thing I'll adjust next week?

WEEK 23: THE PLATEAU
WHEN YOUR LEARNING CURVE SEEMS TO FLATTEN

Welcome to the plateau. You've been working consistently for months now. Your rituals are solid. You keep showing up. But maybe progress that felt rapid early on has slowed to a crawl. This feeling—that you're putting in effort without seeing equivalent returns—is completely normal around this time. This is the plateau—it's not a dead end.

The Research: Plateaus in Skill Acquisition

Research on learning and performance shows that plateaus are not indicators of failure—they're part of the natural learning curve. When you first start a new skill or behavior, progress feels rapid. Your brain is building new neural pathways, and every repetition creates noticeable improvement. As you advance, the improvements become more subtle. You're no longer learning the basics—you're refining, deepening, consolidating. The gains are still happening—they're just harder to detect because they're incremental rather than dramatic. Psychologist Anders Ericsson's research on expertise shows that plateaus are actually periods of consolidation. Your brain is integrating what you've learned, preparing for the next leap.

The Plateau Is Fertile Ground

Think of it like this: after a seed sprouts and grows its first leaves, there's often a period where visible growth above ground slows dramatically. That's not stagnation—that's the plant focusing energy on developing a stronger root system underground.

The roots spread wider. The stem thickens. The foundation strengthens. All of this is invisible progress, but it's what allows the plant to support larger leaves, taller growth, and eventually flowers and fruit.

You're not stuck, you're catching your breath for the next growth spurt.

THIS WEEK'S FOCUS

→ **Identify one skill or aspect of your ritual that has subtly improved. Maybe your form is better. Maybe it takes less mental effort to start. Maybe you recover faster when you miss.**

→ **Acknowledge the hidden work. Write down three ways you've grown that aren't visible in outcomes—patience, resilience, self-trust, consistency.**

→ **Commit to sticking with your rituals. The breakthrough happens only if you ride the plateau long enough. The next surge will come!**

PROGRESS TRACKER

GOAL # 1
RITUALS:

....

Scheduled for:
....
Accomplished:
....

GOAL # 2
RITUALS:

....

Scheduled for:
....
Accomplished:
....

GOAL # 3
RITUALS:

....

Scheduled for:
....
Accomplished:
....

THIS WEEK'S INSIGHTS AND LEARNINGS

What did this week teach me?

....

What's one achievement I'm proud of?

....

What's one thing I'll adjust next week?

....

Week 24: Reconnecting With Your Why
Keep the Motivation Flowing Even When Your Purpose Shifts

Back in Week 2, you dug deep to find your "why." You asked yourself five times: "Why does this matter?" You defined the purpose that got you started. It carried you through the first dip. It anchored you when motivation faded.

Now it's time to check in again. Has your "why" deepened? Shifted? Evolved?

The Research: Motivation as a Dynamic Process

Psychologist Edward Deci's research on self-determination theory shows that motivation isn't static—it evolves as we grow.

Early on, motivation might be more extrinsic: "I want to look a certain way." "I want to impress others." "I want to prove I can do this."

Over time, as behavior becomes internalized, motivation often shifts toward intrinsic alignment: "This feels true to who I am." "I do this because it matters to me, not because I need to prove anything."

That shift is a sign of growth. Your "why" deepening is evidence that you're changing.

Has Your Motivation Shifted?

Ask yourself:

- *Am I still doing this for the same reasons I started?*
- *Has my relationship with this goal evolved?*
- *What drives me now—ego or alignment?*

There's no right answer. But awareness matters.

This Week's Focus

→ **Reread your Week 2 reflections. Does your "why" still resonate? Has it changed?**

→ **Write a new version if needed. Let it reflect what drives you toward achieving your goals.**

→ **Remember: Clarity about your purpose will help you stay consistent when the next plateau hits.**

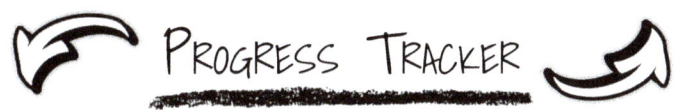

PROGRESS TRACKER

GOAL # 1
RITUALS:
....

Scheduled for:
....

Accomplished:
....

GOAL # 2
RITUALS:
....

Scheduled for:
....

Accomplished:
....

GOAL # 3
RITUALS:
....

Scheduled for:
....

Accomplished:
....

THIS WEEK'S INSIGHTS AND LEARNINGS

What did this week teach me?
....

What's one achievement I'm proud of?
....

What's one thing I'll adjust next week?
....

WEEK 25: PLAYFULNESS IN PRACTICE
REDISCOVERING JOY IN THE JOURNEY

You've been showing up for months—building rituals, navigating dips, adjusting with care. That's serious dedication, and it deserves celebration.

But when was the last time you actually enjoyed your ritual? When did you laugh halfway through, feel light instead of obligated, or let it be fun instead of just "productive"?

The Research: Why Play Sustains Motivation

Psychiatrist Stuart Brown shows that play is a core human drive tied to creativity, resilience, and persistence. Approaching a task with curiosity or humor triggers dopamine and endorphins that help your brain tag the experience as rewarding — making you far more likely to return. Studies on motivation science confirm it's not discipline *versus* play; it's discipline *with* play that lasts longest. People who enjoy the process maintain habits up to 40 % longer than those focused only on results.

Playfulness isn't abandoning your rituals. It's bringing a lighter energy into them — turning "have to" into "get to."

What Playfulness Looks Like in Practice

Playfulness works best when the stakes stay low, the routine feels a little new, and the wins are celebrated right away. Here are some ideas for inspiration. Keep the ritual, change the feel.

- *Task Bowl: Write five tiny tasks on slips; draw one, do it.*
- *One Song Warmup: Start your ritual with your favorite energizing track.*
- *Single Album Session: One album = one work/study block; stop when it ends.*
- *Location Swap: Same ritual, different environment (window seat, local café, park bench)*

Joy isn't a detour from growth. It's the fuel that keeps you moving—lightly, and longer.

THIS WEEK'S FOCUS

→ **Add one playful element to your existing ritual (music, setting, small challenge).**

→ **Run it with zero pressure. Don't track or optimize — just notice what feels good.**

→ **Mark the win immediately (a loud "Yes!", a stretch, a literal two-second dance).**

PROGRESS TRACKER

GOAL # 1
RITUALS:
....

Scheduled for:
....

Accomplished:
....

GOAL # 2
RITUALS:
....

Scheduled for:
....

Accomplished:
....

GOAL # 3
RITUALS:
....

Scheduled for:
....

Accomplished:
....

THIS WEEK'S INSIGHTS AND LEARNINGS

What did this week teach me?
....

What's one achievement I'm proud of?
....

What's one thing I'll adjust next week?
....

50% MILESTONE REFLECTION
You're Halfway There

Let's Talk About What You've Accomplished.

Think about where you were twenty-five weeks ago. You were just beginning. The year stretched out ahead of you, full of possibility and uncertainty. Now, you're standing at the halfway point—and that matters more than you might realize. How do you feel?

Why the Middle Is the Hardest

Behavioral scientists have identified a phenomenon called the "second-quarter slump" — the period between 25-40% completion when motivation and engagement drop significantly.

But, here's the good news: Studies on long-term goal pursuit show that **reaching the midpoint is the single biggest predictor of completion**. Why? Because you've crossed a psychological threshold. You're no longer in the early stages where quitting feels like giving up on a dream. You're in the territory where quitting would mean abandoning something you've already built—something real, something yours.

You've proven you can sustain change through the hardest phase. You've weathered the motivation dip, the plateau, the doubt. You've shown up on days when it felt pointless. You've returned after missing. You've kept going when no one was watching and nothing felt exciting.

That's proof you can finish what you start.

Many people quit during this valley because they can't see evidence that their effort is paying off. They've been working for months, and the results still feel distant.
Not you, though. You're ready to see your efforts showing results.
And they will - very soon!

Before you move into the next season, use this week to assess where you are. Again, not judgmental, but with curiosity - to help you prepare for the next 12 weeks.

Complete the following 5 steps. Like last time, decide if you want to do one each day to stay, split them over 2 or 3 days, or answer them all in one go. You know yourself best.

Step 1: Review Your Goals and Milestones

Go back to the **Goals**. For each one, ask yourself:

- *Does this goal still feel aligned with who I want to become?*
- *Has anything shifted that requires adjustment?*

It's okay if your goals have evolved. You're not locked in.

Goal #1

Goal #2

Goal #3

Now look at your **Milestones** for each.

- *Did you achieve them?*
- *Exceed them?*
- *Fall short?*

All outcomes provide valuable learning. If you exceeded expectations, consider setting a higher target for the next season. If you fell short, ask yourself why—and whether your next milestone needs to be more realistic.

Goal #1: 50% Milestone ☐ *achieved* ☐ *exceeded* ☐ *fell short*
My 75% Milestone will be:

Goal #2: 50% Milestone ☐ *achieved* ☐ *exceeded* ☐ *fell short*
My 75% Milestone will be:

Goal #3: 50% Milestone ☐ *achieved* ☐ *exceeded* ☐ *fell short*
My 75% Milestone will be:

Step 2: Identify Your Patterns

You've gathered another twelve weeks of data about yourself. Awareness is the first step to change. When you acknowledge your patterns, you can align your rhythm with them.

When do you show up most consistently?
Time of day, day of week, circumstances?

When do you struggle most?
What triggers make it harder?

What helps you return after missing?
What Mindset, strategy, or support gets you back on track?

Step 3: Develop Your Next Rituals

For your Bloom Season's milestones, design rituals that leverage what you've learned about yourself. Make them specific, and make them sustainable.

Goal #1: 75% Milestone

Weekly Rituals →
→
→

Goal #2: 75% Milestone

Weekly Rituals →
→
→

Goal #3: 75% Milestone

Weekly Rituals →
→
→

Step 4: Acknowledge Your Wins

Write at least three things you're genuinely proud of from the past 12 weeks.

Like last time, don't look for the big achievements. Acknowledge even the smallest of tasks well performed.

....

....

....

....

Step 5: Set One Intention for the Next Season

Your upcoming Bloom Season is about recognizing growth that's becoming visible. Your rituals are shifting from effortful to automatic. This season helps you own your transformation and navigate becoming someone new. What's one thing you want to focus on in the next 12 weeks?

Examples:

- *"I want to recognize my progress without needing external validation."*
- *"I want to own my transformation publicly."*
- *"I want to deepen my practice without burning out."*

....

My intention for the next season:

....

....

A Note Before Moving Forward

The upcoming Bloom Season will feel different from the first two. Something is shifting. Your rituals may be feeling less like effort and more like who you are. Some days, you might notice changes you didn't expect. That's growth becoming visible.

Remember: You've already navigated the hardest part—the messy middle. You've stayed when most people quit. You've proven you can sustain change even when it's hard. Keep going. Now comes the time when transformation becomes undeniable.

WEEK 27: THE SHIFT YOU DIDN'T NOTICE
RECOGNIZING INCREMENTAL CHANGE

Remember the bamboo metaphor from Week 19? Now is the time your roots are strong and the shoots start emerging - but are you noticing it? Transformation doesn't announce itself with fanfare. It happens so gradually that your brain adapts in real time, making the changes invisible to you even as they're becoming undeniable to everyone else. This week is about learning to see what's already shifted.

The Research: The Aggregation of Marginal Gains

British cycling coach Dave Brailsford popularized a concept called "the aggregation of marginal gains." His philosophy: if you improve every aspect of performance by just 1%, the cumulative effect is transformative. This approach catapulted British cycling from mediocrity to dominance.

Research on habit formation supports this. Small, consistent actions compound over time. Each repetition strengthens neural pathways. Each choice reinforces identity. Each day builds on the last.

The problem? Our brains are terrible at recognizing gradual change. Psychologist Daniel Kahneman's research on adaptation shows that humans are wired to notice novelty, not consistency. Once something becomes familiar, it becomes invisible—even when it represents massive growth.

The 1% Shifts You've Already Made

If you've been showing up consistently, here's what's likely different now—even if you haven't noticed:

- *Your rituals require less mental effort to start.*
  What once took willpower now happens almost automatically.
- *You recover faster when you miss.*
  Returning after a setback doesn't feel as heavy as it once did.
- *You have proof.*
  Months ago, you hoped you could change. Now there's evidence that you already have.

These aren't small things. They're the foundation of everything.

THIS WEEK'S FOCUS

→ **Identify one ritual that could improve by just 1% this week. Start 2 minutes earlier. Add one extra rep. Choose a slightly healthier option.**

→ **Ask someone close to you what they've noticed about you lately. Their answer might surprise you. Other people often see your growth before you do.**

→ **Give yourself credit for the invisible work. You've been building roots for months. The fact that growth feels automatic now isn't a sign nothing's happening—it's a sign everything is working.**

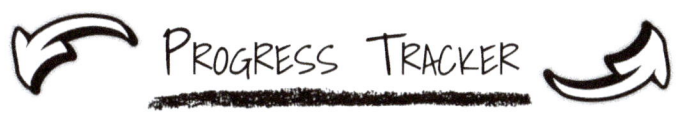

PROGRESS TRACKER

GOAL # 1
RITUALS:

....

Scheduled for:
....

Accomplished:
....

GOAL # 2
RITUALS:

....

Scheduled for:
....

Accomplished:
....

GOAL # 3
RITUALS:

....

Scheduled for:
....

Accomplished:
....

THIS WEEK'S INSIGHTS AND LEARNINGS

What did this week teach me?

....

What's one achievement I'm proud of?

....

What's one thing I'll adjust next week?

....

WEEK 28: OWNING YOUR GROWTH
CLAIMING YOUR PROGRESS WITHOUT APOLOGIZING

You're officially closer to the finish line than you are to the starting point now. Yay! But when someone compliments your progress, what do you say?

If you're like most people, you probably downplay it: "Oh, it's nothing." "I still have a long way to go." "I've just been lucky."

This week is about learning to own your growth—without shrinking, without apologizing, without waiting for permission.

The Research: Imposter Syndrome and Self-Sabotage

Psychologist Pauline Clance's research on imposter syndrome reveals that high-achieving people often struggle to internalize their accomplishments. They attribute success to luck, timing, or external factors—never to their own effort or ability.
This pattern doesn't just diminish confidence. It actively undermines future progress. When you refuse to claim your wins, your brain doesn't register them as evidence of capability. The narrative stays stuck: "I'm still not good enough."

Luckily, research on self-affirmation shows the opposite holds true as well: when people acknowledge their growth out loud, it strengthens their belief in their ability to continue growing.

The Power of Saying "I'm Proud of Myself"

It might feel unfamiliar - maybe even a bit uncomfortable. It might seem arrogant. But there's a difference between pride and arrogance.

- *Arrogance says, "I'm better than you."*
- *Pride says, "I worked hard, and I'm honoring that."*

You've earned the right to be proud. Recognize your growth and learn to enjoy the feeling.

THIS WEEK'S FOCUS

→ **Fill in the blank:**

"I am proud of myself for _____"

Pick something you've done consistently - that may have felt impossible six months ago.

→ **Say out loud - to yourself in the mirror, or to your partner. Or, text it to a friend.**

→ **Let it sink in. Enjoy the feeling of accomplishment. You've earned this.**

PROGRESS TRACKER

GOAL # 1
RITUALS:
....
Scheduled for:
....
Accomplished:
....

GOAL # 2
RITUALS:
....
Scheduled for:
....
Accomplished:
....

GOAL # 3
RITUALS:
....
Scheduled for:
....
Accomplished:
....

THIS WEEK'S INSIGHTS AND LEARNINGS

What did this week teach me?
....

What's one achievement I'm proud of?
....

What's one thing I'll adjust next week?
....

Week 29: When Others Don't Understand
Staying Grounded When Your Growth Makes Others Uncomfortable

As you continue to grow, the responses from people around you will vary. Some will celebrate your transformation—they'll notice the shift, cheer you on, and ask how you did it. But others may feel threatened. They'll minimize your progress or remind you of who you used to be. And that can shake you—especially if those people are close to you.

When this happens, remember: their reactions say more about them than about you. Everyone is on their own journey, moving at their own pace. Try not to judge them for their discomfort—but don't shrink to make them comfortable either.

The Research: Why Your Growth Triggers Others

Psychologist Abraham Maslow studied self-actualization and growth resistance. His findings: when one person in a relationship changes, it disrupts the equilibrium. The other person may unconsciously resist that change—not out of malice, but out of discomfort. Your growth can mirror their stagnation. Your discipline can highlight their avoidance. Your consistency can make them feel left behind.

Research on social identity theory shows that when someone evolves beyond their established role in a group, it can trigger defensiveness in others who are still attached to the old dynamic. This isn't about blame. It's about awareness. Your transformation doesn't require their approval.

Setting Boundaries Without Defensiveness

You don't need to explain yourself. You don't need to convince anyone that your growth is valid. But you do need to protect it.

That might mean limiting conversations about your goals with people who diminish them. It might mean spending less time with people who need you to stay small. It might mean saying, kindly but firmly: "This matters to me. I'd appreciate your support—but I'm doing this regardless."

This Week's Focus

→ **Reconnect with your energy givers (revisit Week 21).**
Invest time with people who celebrate your growth, not those who resist it.

→ **Set one boundary if needed—with compassion. Protect your growth without making others wrong. "This really matters to me" is often enough.**

→ **Let people be where they are. Focus your energy on building a community that lifts you higher, not convincing those who don't understand.**

PROGRESS TRACKER

GOAL # 1
RITUALS:

....

Scheduled for:

....

Accomplished:

....

GOAL # 2
RITUALS:

....

Scheduled for:

....

Accomplished:

....

GOAL # 3
RITUALS:

....

Scheduled for:

....

Accomplished:

....

THIS WEEK'S INSIGHTS AND LEARNINGS

What did this week teach me?

....

What's one achievement I'm proud of?

....

What's one thing I'll adjust next week?

....

Week 30: The Temptation to Quit
Why Success Can Feel Scary

Here's a strange paradox: the closer you get to real change, the stronger the urge to self-sabotage.

You're 30 weeks in. Things are working. Rituals feel natural. Progress is visible. And suddenly, you're tempted to stop. Not because you're failing. Because you're succeeding, and success comes with its own kind of fear.

The Research: Upper Limit Problems

Psychologist Gay Hendricks identified a phenomenon he calls "upper limit problems"—the unconscious ways we sabotage ourselves when we approach a new level of success, happiness, or growth.

His research shows that most people have an internal thermostat for how much success they believe they're allowed to experience. When they exceed that threshold, they unconsciously create problems to bring themselves back down.

Why? Because staying in familiar territory—even if it's uncomfortable—feels safer than stepping into the unknown.

Neuroscience supports this. Your brain is wired to prioritize predictability over possibility. Change, even positive change, registers as a threat.

The Fear of Becoming Someone New

If you succeed at this, you become someone different. And that comes with questions:

- *Will people still relate to me?*
- *What if I can't sustain this?*
- *What if this new version of me isn't who I thought I'd be?*

These fears are normal. And they often show up right before a breakthrough.

This Week's Focus

→ **If you're tempted to stop now - or at any point in the future - ask yourself:**
   "What am I afraid will happen if I keep going?"

→ **Write down the fear.** _____
   Look at it. Then ask: "Is this fear protecting me—or holding me back?"

You've come too far to let fear win now - or ever!

PROGRESS TRACKER

GOAL # 1
RITUALS:
....
Scheduled for:
....
Accomplished:
....

GOAL # 2
RITUALS:
....
Scheduled for:
....
Accomplished:
....

GOAL # 3
RITUALS:
....
Scheduled for:
....
Accomplished:
....

★ THIS WEEK'S INSIGHTS AND LEARNINGS ★

What did this week teach me?
....

What's one achievement I'm proud of?
....

What's one thing I'll adjust next week?
....

WEEK 31: INTEGRATION, NOT PERFECTION
MAKING PEACE WITH INCONSISTENCY

Thirty weeks in, and you've probably noticed something: you still have off days. Even now. Some weeks, your rituals feel effortless. Other weeks, you struggle. You miss. You adjust. You return. And you might be wondering: "Shouldn't this be easier by now?"

Here's the truth: growth is not linear—it never will be.

The Research: The Myth of Linear Progress

Research on skill acquisition and behavior change consistently shows that progress follows a pattern called "punctuated equilibrium"—periods of stability interrupted by sudden bursts of growth, followed by plateaus, then more growth.

Psychologist K. Anders Ericsson's studies on expertise reveal that even masters have inconsistent performance. The difference isn't that they never struggle—it's that they've made peace with the struggle. They don't interpret a bad day as evidence that they're failing. They see it as part of the natural rhythm of growth.

Your takeaway? Practice self-compassion: treating yourself with the same kindness you'd offer a close friend. According to research by Dr. Kristin Neff, this is one of the strongest predictors of sustained behavior change.

Self-Compassion as a Success Strategy

People who practice self-compassion are more likely to return after setbacks, more resilient in the face of challenges, and less likely to quit when things feel hard.

Perfectionism, on the other hand, is correlated with higher rates of burnout and abandonment.

THIS WEEK'S FOCUS

→ **Practice self-compassion when struggle shows up.** The next time a ritual feels hard or you miss a day, speak to yourself like you would to a friend. Replace "I'm failing" with "It's ok. This is part of the process."

→ **Make peace with the struggle (revisit Week 9).** Inconsistency isn't evidence of failure—it's proof you're human. What matters is how quickly you return, not how perfectly you performed.

→ **Notice one way you've been kinder to yourself.** Are you judging yourself less harshly than you did in Week 1? That shift—however small—is integration happening in real time.

PROGRESS TRACKER

GOAL # 1
RITUALS:
....
Scheduled for:
....
Accomplished:
....

GOAL # 2
RITUALS:
....
Scheduled for:
....
Accomplished:
....

GOAL # 3
RITUALS:
....
Scheduled for:
....
Accomplished:
....

THIS WEEK'S INSIGHTS AND LEARNINGS

What did this week teach me?
....

What's one achievement I'm proud of?
....

What's one thing I'll adjust next week?
....

Week 32: What Wants to Bloom Next?
Noticing New Edges of Growth

You've been building rituals around your original goals. Some of those rituals are now automatic. Some are still a work in progress. Now that you are in a nice flow, here's what often happens around this point: something new starts calling to you.

Maybe it's a skill you want to develop. A relationship you want to deepen. A habit you've been avoiding but now feel ready to approach.

This is a sign of growth. When one thing takes root, space opens for something new.

The Research: Expansion Without Overwhelm

Psychologist Mihaly Csikszentmihalyi's research on flow states reveals that humans are naturally drawn to challenge—but only when it's slightly beyond their current ability level. Too easy, and we get bored. Too hard, and we get overwhelmed. The sweet spot is just outside our comfort zone—what he calls "the growth edge."

When rituals become automatic, your brain seeks the next edge. That's not restlessness. That's evolution. But here's the key: expansion works best when it's gradual, not drastic.

Saying Yes to the Next Gentle Edge

You don't need to overhaul your entire routine. You don't need to add three new goals. You just need to notice: what feels like a natural "next"—not because you should, but because you're ready? This might look like:

- *Your morning ritual feels solid. Now, you're curious about adding an evening wind-down practice.*
- *You've been consistent with movement. Now you're drawn to trying a new form of exercise.*
- *Your creative habit has taken root. You're ready to share your work with one trusted person.*
- *You've mastered the basics of a skill. You tackle something slightly more complex.*

The keyword is *gentle*. The next edge shouldn't feel like starting from scratch. It should feel like a natural extension of what you've already built—challenging enough to be interesting, familiar enough to be sustainable.

This Week's Focus

→ **Ask yourself: "What wants to grow next?"**

→ **Not what you think you should do. What genuinely calls to you.**

→ **Write it down. You don't have to act on it yet. Just acknowledge it. Let it simmer.**

PROGRESS TRACKER

GOAL # 1
RITUALS:

....

Scheduled for:

....

Accomplished:

....

GOAL # 2
RITUALS:

....

Scheduled for:

....

Accomplished:

....

GOAL # 3
RITUALS:

....

Scheduled for:

....

Accomplished:

....

THIS WEEK'S INSIGHTS AND LEARNINGS

What did this week teach me?

....

What's one achievement I'm proud of?

....

What's one thing I'll adjust next week?

....

Week 33: Gratitude for the Journey
Appreciating Where You Are, Not Just Where You're Going

You're deep into the bloom season now. And if you're honest, you might still be focused on what's left to accomplish. "I still need to…", "I'm not quite there yet…", "Once I reach…"

But here's the question: when was the last time you paused to appreciate where you already are?

The Research: Gratitude and Sustained Motivation

Dr. Robert Emmons, the leading researcher on gratitude, has spent decades studying its effects on well-being and motivation. His findings: people who practice gratitude regularly report higher levels of sustained motivation, greater resilience in the face of setbacks, and increased satisfaction with their progress. But here's the key insight: gratitude works best when it's focused on the process, not just the outcome.

Thanking yourself for showing up matters more than celebrating achievements. Appreciating the journey creates more lasting fulfillment than reaching the destination.

Research on hedonic adaptation shows that outcome-based satisfaction fades quickly. You reach a goal, feel good briefly, then your baseline resets. But process-based gratitude—appreciating the daily practice, the growth, the learning—sustains you long-term.

The Trap of "I'll Be Happy When…"

Most people defer happiness: "I'll feel proud when I reach my goal." "I'll celebrate when I see results." "I'll be satisfied when…"

Feeling gratitude is an uplifting and powerful motivator. Appreciating the journey is just as powerful as celebrating the arrival at the destination.

This Week's Focus

→ **Write down 3 things about this journey you're grateful for right now—even the hard parts. Maybe it's the discipline you've built. The self-knowledge you've gained. The resilience you've discovered.**

1._____ 2. _____ 3. _____

Gratitude for where you are doesn't diminish where you're going. It makes the journey worthwhile.

PROGRESS TRACKER

GOAL # 1
RITUALS:
....
Scheduled for:
....
Accomplished:
....

GOAL # 2
RITUALS:
....
Scheduled for:
....
Accomplished:
....

GOAL # 3
RITUALS:
....
Scheduled for:
....
Accomplished:
....

THIS WEEK'S INSIGHTS AND LEARNINGS

What did this week teach me?

....

What's one achievement I'm proud of?

....

What's one thing I'll adjust next week?

....

WEEK 34: DEEPENING THE PRACTICE
MOVING FROM AUTOMATIC TO INTENTIONAL

Thirty-four weeks ago, you started building rituals. You made them small. You made them consistent. You made them stick. And here's the beautiful part: by calling them rituals from the beginning—not just habits—you were already treating them as something meaningful. Something worth protecting. Something intentional. Now, some of those rituals have become automatic. You show up without thinking. The behavior feels effortless. But automaticity brings a risk: when something becomes routine, it's easy to lose the presence that made it powerful in the first place. This week is about rekindling that intention—about ensuring your rituals stay alive, not just automatic.

The Research: Mindfulness and Meaning

Psychologist Ellen Langer's studies on mindfulness reveal that "mindless" repetition can lead to disengagement over time. But when we infuse behaviors with intention and presence, they remain rituals—practices that nourish us, not just tasks we complete. The difference is subtle but powerful:

- *Automatic routine: You do it, but you're disconnected*
- *Intentional ritual: You do it with full presence and meaning*

Research on mindfulness and habit formation shows that when we bring full attention to a behavior—even a simple one—it becomes more meaningful, more satisfying, and more sustainable.

Infusing Meaning Into Daily Actions

You've been building rituals all along. This week is about making sure they stay that way. No need to add more time. You just need to add more presence to what you're already doing.

Instead of rushing through your morning routine, pause. Notice how the water feels. Breathe deeply. Acknowledge that you're choosing to care for yourself.

Instead of just checking off your ritual and moving on, take five seconds to feel gratitude for showing up. Small shifts. Big impact.

THIS WEEK'S FOCUS

→ **Which ritual became automatic? Do it with full attention and intention this week.**

→ **Acknowledge completion. Take five seconds to notice how it felt.**

→ **Notice how different it feels when you're fully there - not on auto-pilot, but with full presence and intention.**

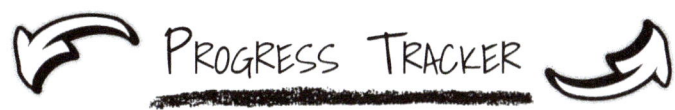

PROGRESS TRACKER

GOAL # 1
RITUALS:
....
Scheduled for:
....
Accomplished:
....

GOAL # 2
RITUALS:
....
Scheduled for:
....
Accomplished:
....

GOAL # 3
RITUALS:
....
Scheduled for:
....
Accomplished:
....

★ THIS WEEK'S INSIGHTS AND LEARNINGS ★

What did this week teach me?
....

What's one achievement I'm proud of?
....

What's one thing I'll adjust next week?
....

WEEK 35: YOUR VALUES
WHAT GUIDES YOU WHEN THINGS GET HARD

You've been building rituals, navigating resistance, and deepening your practice. Some days felt easy. Others required everything you had. Through it all, a powerful force has been guiding you—even if you haven't named it yet. **Your values are the compass that keeps you oriented when motivation fades**, when progress stalls, when life throws unexpected challenges your way. They're not the same as goals. Goals are destinations. Values are the principles that guide how you move through the journey. This week is about bringing those values into focus—so you can lean on them intentionally, especially when things get hard.

The Research: Values-Based Action

Psychologist Steven Hayes, founder of Acceptance and Commitment Therapy (ACT), distinguishes between **goal-directed behavior** and **values-based living**. Goals are finite. You either achieve them or you don't. But values are ongoing—they describe how you want to move through life, regardless of specific outcomes.

Research shows that people who connect their habits to core values experience greater intrinsic motivation, less burnout, and higher rates of sustained behavior change. When your rituals align with your values, they stop feeling like obligations. They become expressions of who you are.

Common Values That Support Growth

Take a moment to consider which of these resonate with you:

- *Discipline — Choosing your future self over your current comfort*
- *Curiosity — Staying open to learning and adjusting*
- *Resilience — Returning after setbacks without shame*
- *Integrity — Keeping promises to yourself*
- *Self-compassion — Treating yourself with kindness through the struggle*
- *Patience — Trusting the process even when progress feels slow*
- *Courage — Showing up even when it's uncomfortable*
- *Authenticity — Staying true to yourself, not performing for others*

You might resonate with several. Or you might have values not listed here. There's no right answer—only what feels true for you.

THIS WEEK'S FOCUS

→ **What value has been guiding me through this journey? Write it down.**

→ **Identify one ritual or connected behavior that directly expresses this value.**
For example, if your value is self-compassion, your ritual of returning without shame after missing embodies that.

→ **When motivation fades, return to your value. Goals can feel distant. Values are always available. They remind you why you started—and why you're still here. When things get hard, your values are what carry you through.**

PROGRESS TRACKER

GOAL # 1
RITUALS:
....
Scheduled for:
....
Accomplished:
....

GOAL # 2
RITUALS:
....
Scheduled for:
....
Accomplished:
....

GOAL # 3
RITUALS:
....
Scheduled for:
....
Accomplished:
....

THIS WEEK'S INSIGHTS AND LEARNINGS

What did this week teach me?
....

What's one achievement I'm proud of?
....

What's one thing I'll adjust next week?
....

Week 36: Handling Change
Navigating Life's Inevitable Shifts

Last week, you identified the values guiding your journey. Those values are your internal compass—stable, reliable, always available. But life itself? Life is anything but stable.

Over the past thirty-five weeks, things have probably shifted. Maybe your schedule changed. Maybe a relationship evolved. Maybe an unexpected challenge appeared. Maybe your priorities reorganized themselves without you planning for it. Change is inevitable. The question isn't whether it will happen—it's how you'll navigate it without losing the momentum you've built.

The Research: Adaptability and Resilience

Research on psychological resilience shows that the most successful people aren't those who avoid change—they're the ones who've developed flexibility in the face of it. Psychologist Carol Dweck's research shows that people with a **growth mindset** see change as an opportunity to adapt, learn, and recalibrate. People with a fixed mindset see change as a disruption that derails progress.

Dr. Dennis Charney's studies on resilience reveal a common trait among highly resilient individuals: they have systems in place that bend without breaking. They adjust their approach while staying anchored to their core values. And that's exactly the key: your values remain constant. Your strategies can flex.

Your Change Response Pattern

Some people thrive on change. It energizes them. They see it as an adventure, an opportunity to try something new. Others need stability and routine. Change feels destabilizing, even threatening. They require time and intentionality to adjust. Neither is right nor wrong. But knowing your pattern helps you navigate change more effectively.

If you're *energized* by change, your challenge is maintaining consistency when the novelty wears off. Anchor yourself to rituals that provide stability.

If you *resist* change, your challenge is staying flexible when life shifts. Remind yourself that adjusting your approach doesn't mean abandoning your commitment.

This Week's Focus

→ **How do you respond to change?**

→ **Identify one strategy that's helped you stay grounded when life felt uncertain.**
Maybe it was returning to your values. Maybe it was shrinking your ritual to the two-minute version. Maybe it was asking for support.
Write it down. It will come in handy when life shifts again next time.

→ **Remember: Your values anchor you. Your flexibility sustains you. Both are essential.**

PROGRESS TRACKER

GOAL # 1
RITUALS:

Scheduled for:

Accomplished:

GOAL # 2
RITUALS:

Scheduled for:

Accomplished:

GOAL # 3
RITUALS:

Scheduled for:

Accomplished:

THIS WEEK'S INSIGHTS AND LEARNINGS

What did this week teach me?

What's one achievement I'm proud of?

What's one thing I'll adjust next week?

WEEK 37: THE STORIES OTHERS TELL ABOUT YOU
RECLAIMING YOUR NARRATIVE

You've grounded yourself in your values. You've learned to navigate change without losing momentum. And through it all, you've been evolving. But here's what happens as you grow: the people around you will update their perception of you—sometimes quickly, sometimes slowly, and sometimes not at all. Some will celebrate the shifts they see. Others will still describe you based on who you were months ago, a year ago, or even longer. And when that happens, you'll need to decide: do I accept their outdated story, or do I gently correct it?

The Research: Identity Negotiation

Sociologist Erving Goffman studied how identities are constructed through social interaction. His research shows that our sense of self is constantly negotiated between how we see ourselves and how others see us. When there's a mismatch—when you've evolved but others still see the old version—it creates cognitive dissonance. You can either shrink back into the old identity to maintain harmony, or you can claim the new one, even if it disrupts expectations. Research on self-verification theory shows that people have a deep need to be seen accurately. When others misperceive us, it doesn't just feel uncomfortable—it can undermine our progress if we don't address it.

Updating Your Story With Others

You don't need to announce your transformation. But you do need to stop agreeing with narratives that no longer fit. When someone says, "But you've always been [old identity]," you can respond gently: "I used to be. I'm becoming something different now."

When someone describes you in a way that feels outdated, you can kindly correct them: "That's not really true for me anymore."

It's not about convincing them. It's about not letting their old story erase your new reality.

THIS WEEK'S FOCUS

→ Notice if someone describes you in a way that no longer fits. Don't ignore it. Gently correct them—not defensively, just honestly.

→ Practice saying: "I'm becoming something different now." It doesn't need to be dramatic. It just needs to be true.

→ Remind yourself: You don't need permission to evolve. Others will catch up when they're ready. Your job is to keep living into the person you're becoming. You're allowed to outgrow old stories—including the ones others tell about you.

PROGRESS TRACKER

GOAL # 1
RITUALS:
....
Scheduled for:
....
Accomplished:
....

GOAL # 2
RITUALS:
....
Scheduled for:
....
Accomplished:
....

GOAL # 3
RITUALS:
....
Scheduled for:
....
Accomplished:
....

★ THIS WEEK'S INSIGHTS AND LEARNINGS ★

What did this week teach me?
....

What's one achievement I'm proud of?
....

What's one thing I'll adjust next week?
....

WEEK 38: LEARNING TOGETHER
THE POWER OF SHARED GROWTH

You've clarified your values. You've learned to navigate change. You've reclaimed your narrative from outdated stories. All of this work has been deeply personal—and much of it has probably been solo. Just you and your rituals, day after day, quietly building something real. Here's something additional worth considering as you approach the final stretch: what if growth didn't have to be lonely

The Research: Social Learning Theory

Research shows that learning with others—whether it's a skill, a habit, or a mindset shift—amplifies motivation, deepens understanding, and increases the likelihood of long-term success. Psychologist Albert Bandura's social learning theory shows that we learn not just from our own experiences, but from observing and engaging with others. When you see someone else working toward a similar goal, it normalizes the struggle. When you share your progress with someone, it reinforces your commitment. When you learn something new together, it creates connection and accountability. Studies on group-based behavior change programs consistently show higher completion rates than solo efforts—not because group work is inherently better, but because shared commitment creates a sense of "we're in this together."

What Shared Growth Could Look Like

You don't need to join a formal group or program. Shared growth can be simple:

- *Finding one person working on a complementary goal and checking in weekly*
- *Teaching someone else a skill you're developing (teaching deepens your own learning)*
- *Joining an online community focused on your area of growth*
- *Inviting someone to try a new experience with you*

You've proven you can do this alone. But inviting others in might make the journey richer.

THIS WEEK'S FOCUS

→ **Is there someone in your life who might benefit from growing alongside you? Not someone you need to convince—someone who's already curious, already moving in a similar direction.**

→ **Reach out. Share what you're working on. Invite them to join you. Remember: You don't have to do this alone. You've built incredible strength through solo work. But community can amplify what you've already created.**

→ **You've come so far on your own. Imagine what's possible when you're not alone anymore.**

PROGRESS TRACKER

GOAL # 1
RITUALS:

Scheduled for:

Accomplished:

GOAL # 2
RITUALS:

Scheduled for:

Accomplished:

GOAL # 3
RITUALS:

Scheduled for:

Accomplished:

THIS WEEK'S INSIGHTS AND LEARNINGS

What did this week teach me?

What's one achievement I'm proud of?

What's one thing I'll adjust next week?

75% MILESTONE REFLECTION
Look at You Blooming

Let's talk about what you've accomplished.

Thirty-eight weeks ago, you decided to commit to something that mattered. You defined your goals. You built your rituals. You showed up. And now, you're here. Three-quarters of the way through your year.

You've moved through three complete seasons. You've planted, nurtured, and watched things bloom. You've proven you can start, persist through the middle, and keep going when the work becomes quiet. Each week, you've added another layer of evidence that transformation isn't a moment—it's a practice.

What you've built over these thirty-eight weeks isn't fragile anymore. It's woven into who you are.

Why This Milestone Matters

Behavioral economists have identified something called "the final quarter effect"—a phenomenon where motivation and performance increase as people approach the end of a goal period. Research also shows that when people perceive they're nearing completion, they experience a surge of energy and focus. The finish line becomes visible, and suddenly, effort feels more meaningful.

But here's the critical part: this effect only kicks in if people have stayed engaged long enough to reach the final stretch. You've done that. You've built enough momentum that the finish line is real—not hypothetical.

You're standing in rare territory. Most people who start a year-long commitment never make it this far. But you have.

You're no longer wondering if you can sustain change. You're living proof that you already have.

Before you move into the next season, use this week to assess where you are. You know the drill by now: Do not judge—create clarity about how to move on.

Complete the following 5 steps at your own pace.

Step 1: Review Your Goals and Milestones

Go back to the *goals* you set in the introduction. For each one, ask yourself:

- *Does this goal still feel aligned with who I want to become?*
- *Has anything shifted that requires adjustment?*

It's okay if your goals have evolved. You're not locked in.

Goal #1

Goal #2

Goal #3

Now look at your *milestones* for each.

- *Did you achieve them?*
- *Exceed them?*
- *Fall short?*

All outcomes provide valuable learning. If you exceeded expectations, consider setting a higher target for the next season. If you fell short, ask yourself why—and whether your next milestone needs to be more realistic.

Goal #1: 25% Milestone ☐ *achieved*   ☐ *exceeded*   ☐ *fell short*
My 50% Milestone will be:

Goal #2: 25% Milestone ☐ *achieved*   ☐ *exceeded*   ☐ *fell short*
My 50% Milestone will be:

Goal #3: 25% Milestone ☐ *achieved*   ☐ *exceeded*   ☐ *fell short*
My 50% Milestone will be:

Step 2: Identify Your Patterns

You've gathered twelve more weeks of data about yourself. Awareness is the first step to change. When you acknowledge your patterns, you can align your rhythm with them.

....

When do you show up most consistently?
Time of day, day of week, circumstances?

....

When do you struggle most?
What triggers make it harder?

....

What helps you return after missing?
What Mindset, strategy, or support gets you back on track?

....

Step 3: Develop Your Next Rituals

For your Harvest Season's milestones, design rituals that leverage what you've learned about yourself. Make them specific, and make them sustainable.

....

Goal #1: 100% Milestone

....

Weekly Rituals →

→

→

....
....

Goal #2: 100% Milestone

....

Weekly Rituals →

→

→

....
....

Goal #3: 100% Milestone

....

Weekly Rituals →

→

→

....

Step 4: Acknowledge Your Wins

Write at least three things you're genuinely proud of from the past 12 weeks. These don't need to be dramatic. "I showed up even when I didn't feel like it" is a massive win. "I returned the day after missing" counts. "I didn't judge myself when I struggled" is growth. Name your victories—no matter how small they feel.

....

....

....

....

Step 5: Set One Intention for the Next Season

Your upcoming Harvest Season is about integration and reflection. You're not racing toward a finish line—you're gathering what you've learned, celebrating what worked, and preparing to sustain your growth beyond this framework. What's one thing you want to focus on in the next 12 weeks?

Examples:

- *"I want to identify what I'll carry forward after Week 52."*
- *"I want to celebrate how far I've come without diminishing it."*
- *"I want to feel complete, not just finished."*

....

My intention for the next season:

....

....

A Note Before Moving Forward

The upcoming Harvest Season is different from the others. It's not about building or pushing or proving. It's about gathering, reflecting, and integrating. Your rituals are now part of who you are—they're not something you do, they're something you live.

Remember: You've already done what most people never do. You've sustained change through every season, every challenge, every moment of doubt. You've proven transformation isn't a sprint—it's a practice.

WEEK 40: WHAT YOU'RE RELEASING
LETTING GO WITH GRATITUDE

Welcome to the final season: the Harvest. You've planted, nurtured, and bloomed. Now comes the work of gathering—not just what you've grown, but also recognizing what you're ready to let go of. Growth isn't only about addition. It's also about release. Over the past weeks and months, some things have naturally fallen away. Old habits that didn't serve you. Beliefs that limited you. Expectations that no longer fit who you're becoming. This week is about acknowledging those releases—and honoring them with gratitude for what they once gave you.

The Research: The Necessity of Letting Go

Research on psychological flexibility shows that one of the key markers of mental health and well-being is the ability to let go of what no longer serves you—without guilt, resentment, or attachment.

Psychologist Susan David's work on emotional agility emphasizes that growth requires releasing old patterns, even when they once protected or comforted us. Clinging to what worked in the past prevents you from stepping into what's possible now.

Studies on habit replacement reveal that sustainable change often requires not just building new behaviors, but actively releasing old ones. You can't hold onto everything and still evolve.

What Release Looks Like

Some releases were intentional. You chose to stop doing something that wasn't working. Some releases were natural. As you grew, certain things simply fell away without you needing to force them. Both deserve gratitude. What once served you—even if it was limiting—helped you get here. But it doesn't need to come with you into the next season. Letting go isn't a loss. It's making space for what matters most.

THIS WEEK'S FOCUS

→ **Identify one thing you've released over the past months.**
A limiting belief? A ritual that didn't stick? A relationship dynamic that no longer fits?

→ **Write a brief thank-you to it (mentally, on paper, or a note on your phone)**
Acknowledge what it gave you when you needed it. Then let it go, knowing that releasing it was part of your growth.

→ **Notice what space has opened up. When you release what's complete, you make room for what wants to grow next.**

PROGRESS TRACKER

GOAL # 1
RITUALS:

....

Scheduled for:

....

Accomplished:

....

GOAL # 2
RITUALS:

....

Scheduled for:

....

Accomplished:

....

GOAL # 3
RITUALS:

....

Scheduled for:

....

Accomplished:

....

THIS WEEK'S INSIGHTS AND LEARNINGS

What did this week teach me?

....

What's one achievement I'm proud of?

....

What's one thing I'll adjust next week?

....

WEEK 41: SUSTAINING WITHOUT STRIVING
MAINTENANCE IS NOT STAGNATION

Last week, you acknowledged what you've released. Now, let's focus on what remains—and how to keep it alive without exhausting yourself. You've been busy building. You've planted seeds, nurtured growth, and watched things bloom. But now comes a different kind of work: sustaining. And here's what no one tells you: sustaining can feel less exciting than building. There's no novelty. No dramatic milestones. No surge of motivation pushing you forward. But sustaining is where real transformation lives. It's the quiet commitment to keep going—not because it's thrilling, but because it's become part of who you are.

The Research: The Transition From Building to Maintaining

Behavioral psychologist James Prochaska's *Transtheoretical Model of Change* identifies distinct stages of behavior change. Most people focus on the "action" stage—the phase of active effort and visible progress. But the final stage—"maintenance"—is where most people fail. Why? Because maintenance feels less rewarding. The dopamine hits are smaller. The sense of urgency fades. And without intentional structures, old patterns creep back in.

Research shows that people who successfully maintain long-term change don't rely on motivation. They rely on systems, rhythms, and a shifted identity that makes the behavior feel inevitable, not optional.

Creating Sustainable Rhythms

Sustaining doesn't mean doing everything perfectly forever. It means creating a baseline—a minimum viable version of your rituals that you can maintain even on your lowest-energy days.

What's the smallest version of your ritual that still counts? That's your maintenance mode. When life gets overwhelming, when motivation dips, when energy is scarce—you don't abandon the ritual. You scale it down to the baseline and keep going.

THIS WEEK'S FOCUS

→ **For each ritual, define your maintenance baseline.**
- ✧ What's the full version (when you have time and energy)?
- ✧ What's the minimum version (that still counts)?

→ **On the next low-energy day, do the maintenance version.**
- ✧ Notice how it feels to show up without pressure.

→ **Remind yourself: Maintenance is not stagnation.**
It's choosing consistency over intensity. It's what carries your progress forward.

PROGRESS TRACKER

GOAL # 1
RITUALS:

....

Scheduled for:

....

Accomplished:

....

GOAL # 2
RITUALS:

....

Scheduled for:

....

Accomplished:

....

GOAL # 3
RITUALS:

....

Scheduled for:

....

Accomplished:

....

THIS WEEK'S INSIGHTS AND LEARNINGS

What did this week teach me?

....

What's one achievement I'm proud of?

....

What's one thing I'll adjust next week?

....

Week 42: Living Your Identity
From Becoming to Being

You've released what no longer serves you. You've defined how to sustain what remains. Now comes the most profound shift of all: recognizing that you're no longer becoming someone new. You already *are* that person. Back in Week 37, you reclaimed your narrative — you learned to correct outdated stories others told about you. That was about external claiming: telling the world who you are now.

This week is different. This is about internal knowing: living as that person, without announcement, without needing to prove it.

The Research: Identity Integration

Psychologist William James observed over a century ago that our self-concept often lags behind our actual behavior. We continue to see ourselves as "the person who struggles with consistency" long after we've proven otherwise.

Research on self-perception theory shows that identity change happens slowly—and often, only when we deliberately update the narrative we tell ourselves. Studies by psychologist Phillippa Lally found that even after people successfully maintain a new behavior for months, many still don't identify with that behavior. They see it as something *they do*, not something *they are*. The shift from "I'm trying to be disciplined" to "I am disciplined" is profound. And it requires conscious acknowledgment.

Who Are You Now?

You're not the same person who started this journey. But have you claimed that internally? Do you still introduce yourself using your old identity? Do you still describe yourself based on who you were, not who you've become?

The evidence is clear: you've shown up for forty-two weeks. You've navigated resistance, setbacks, plateaus, and doubt. You've adjusted without quitting. You've returned after missing. That's not someone "trying" to change. That's someone who *has* changed.

This Week's Focus

→ **Complete this sentence—and say it out loud:**

"I am someone who _____**."**
Fill in the blank with something that's now undeniably true about you.

→ **Pay attention to when you use "trying to" language in the next few days, and replace "I'm trying to be more consistent" with "I'm consistent."**
The words shape the identity.

PROGRESS TRACKER

GOAL # 1
RITUALS:
....

Scheduled for:
....

Accomplished:
....

GOAL # 2
RITUALS:
....

Scheduled for:
....

Accomplished:
....

GOAL # 3
RITUALS:
....

Scheduled for:
....

Accomplished:
....

THIS WEEK'S INSIGHTS AND LEARNINGS

What did this week teach me?
....

What's one achievement I'm proud of?
....

What's one thing I'll adjust next week?
....

Week 43: The Wisdom of Seasons
Understanding Cyclical Growth

You've released what's complete. You've defined how to sustain what matters. You've claimed the identity you've built. Now, it's time to zoom out and see the bigger picture: growth doesn't happen in straight lines. It moves in cycles. During your journey so far, you've experienced something important—seasons. There were weeks when everything felt easy. Weeks when nothing worked. Weeks of rapid progress. Weeks of plateau. And all of it—every single phase—was necessary.

The Research: Cyclical Models of Growth

Research on human development, from Erik Erikson's life stages to nature's seasonal rhythms, reveals a fundamental truth: growth happens in cycles, not straight lines. Studies on performance and productivity show that sustainable high achievement requires periods of intensity followed by periods of rest and integration. Athletes call this "*periodization*." Artists call it "*creative cycles*." Farmers call it "*seasons*."

Psychologist Daniel Levinson's research on adult development shows that life moves through alternating periods of stability and transition. Each phase serves a purpose. Trying to stay in growth mode indefinitely leads to burnout. Trying to avoid transition leads to stagnation.

You Will Plant Again. You Will Rest Again.

This book gave you a structure for one year—one full cycle of goal setting and pursuing. But your life will have many cycles.

- *Some seasons will call for planting: new goals, new intentions, new energy.*
- *Some will call for nurturing: patient tending, showing up, trusting invisible progress.*
- *Some seasons will call for blooming: recognition, visibility, celebration.*
- *Some will call for harvest: reflection, integration, gratitude.*
- *And some seasons will call for rest: stillness, recovery, simply enjoying what you've built.*

Neither one is better than the others. All are necessary and essential for sustainable growth.

This Week's Focus

→ **Reflect: What season does my life feel like right now?**
Honor where you are. Grass doesn't grow faster when you pull it.

→ **Trust that the season will shift when it's time.**
Practice patience and mindfully focus on what is required at this very moment..

PROGRESS TRACKER

GOAL # 1
RITUALS:
....
Scheduled for:
....
Accomplished:
....

GOAL # 2
RITUALS:
....
Scheduled for:
....
Accomplished:
....

GOAL # 3
RITUALS:
....
Scheduled for:
....
Accomplished:
....

THIS WEEK'S INSIGHTS AND LEARNINGS

What did this week teach me?
....

What's one achievement I'm proud of?
....

What's one thing I'll adjust next week?
....

Week 44: Redefining Success
What "Winning" Really Means

You understand now that growth moves in cycles. You've learned to honor each season—the planting, the nurturing, the bloom, the harvest, the rest. But here's a question worth sitting with as you near the end of this journey: By your own definition—not anyone else's standards—have you succeeded?

Most people measure success purely by outcomes. Did I achieve the goal? Did I hit the target? Did I get the result I wanted? After all those weeks of showing up, you know something deeper: success isn't just about the destination. It's about how you developed on the journey there.

The Research: Reframing Success

Research on goal achievement distinguishes between outcome-based success and process-based success.

Outcome-based: *"Did I achieve the specific result I set out to accomplish?"*

Process-based: *"Did I show up consistently? Did I grow? Did I become someone new?"*

Studies show that people who measure success by process rather than outcomes report higher satisfaction, greater resilience, and more sustained behavior change. Why? Because outcomes are often beyond your control. The process is entirely within it.

Psychologist Carol Dweck's research on growth mindset reveals that the most successful people don't measure themselves by results alone—they measure themselves by effort, learning, and growth.

What Does Success Mean to You?

By traditional standards, success might mean: hitting every milestone, completing every ritual perfectly, and achieving every goal.

But by a deeper standard, success might mean: showing up more weeks than not, learning how to return after setbacks, and discovering who you're capable of becoming.

Which definition feels truer?

This Week's Focus

→ **Ask yourself: "By my own definition—not by anyone else's standards—have I succeeded?" Answer honestly - mentally or in writing.**

→ **List three ways you've succeeded that have nothing to do with outcomes.**
Maybe you learned patience. Maybe you built resilience. Maybe you proved you're someone who keeps going.

→ **Remember: Success isn't a fixed finish line. You define what it looks like. And looking at how far you came, you're already doing fantastic!**

PROGRESS TRACKER

GOAL # 1
RITUALS:
....
Scheduled for:
....
Accomplished:
....

GOAL # 2
RITUALS:
....
Scheduled for:
....
Accomplished:
....

GOAL # 3
RITUALS:
....
Scheduled for:
....
Accomplished:
....

THIS WEEK'S INSIGHTS AND LEARNINGS

What did this week teach me?
....

What's one achievement I'm proud of?
....

What's one thing I'll adjust next week?
....

WEEK 45: YOUR EXTERNAL CONTRIBUTION
HOW YOUR GROWTH RIPPLES OUTWARD

You've redefined what success means to you. You've measured your journey by your own standards, not external expectations. But here's something you might not have considered: your transformation doesn't just affect you. It ripples outward—whether you realize it or not. Back in Week 38, you explored the power of learning together—inviting others to grow alongside you. That was about intentional collaboration.

This week is different. This is about recognizing the quiet influence you already have, simply by living as someone who's committed to growth.

The Research: Modeling and Social Influence

Psychologist Albert Bandura's research on social learning shows that people don't just learn from direct instruction—they learn by observing others. When someone witnesses another person consistently showing up, changing, and growing, it shifts what they believe is possible for themselves. You don't need to announce your transformation. You don't need to convince anyone of anything. Your actions speak louder than any explanation.

Research on behavioral contagion shows that habits and behaviors spread through social networks—often invisibly. When you commit to growth, the people around you notice. Some consciously, some unconsciously. But they notice.

The Ripple Effect of Your Consistency

Think about the people in your life who've watched you show up for forty-five weeks. Maybe they haven't said anything. Maybe they have. But they've seen you return after missing. They've seen you adjust without quitting. They've seen you become someone who keeps their word to themselves. That matters more than you know.

Your growth gives others permission to believe change is possible. Not because you told them—but because you showed them.

THIS WEEK'S FOCUS

→ **Reflect: Who has witnessed my growth this year?**
Family, friends, coworkers, even strangers who see you at the gym every week.

→ **Acknowledge one way your transformation might have affected someone else.**
Maybe someone asked how you stay consistent. Maybe someone started their own ritual after seeing yours.

→ **Let yourself feel the weight of that.**
Your growth isn't just personal. It's a quiet contribution to everyone around you.

PROGRESS TRACKER

GOAL # 1
RITUALS:
....
Scheduled for:
....
Accomplished:
....

GOAL # 2
RITUALS:
....
Scheduled for:
....
Accomplished:
....

GOAL # 3
RITUALS:
....
Scheduled for:
....
Accomplished:
....

THIS WEEK'S INSIGHTS AND LEARNINGS

What did this week teach me?
....

What's one achievement I'm proud of?
....

What's one thing I'll adjust next week?
....

WEEK 46: THE PRACTICE OF RETURNING
WHAT TO DO WHEN YOU DRIFT

You've recognized how far you've come and defined success on your own terms. You've seen how your growth has rippled outward. But let's be honest about what comes next: at some point after this book ends, you most likely will drift. Not because you're failing. Not because you didn't learn enough. But because life happens, and seasons change, and sometimes we lose our way.

This week is about building your return plan—a roadmap for the inevitable moments when life pulls you away from what matters. And to help you continue after this year concludes.

The Research: Relapse Prevention

Research in addiction recovery and behavior change identifies "**relapse prevention**" as a critical component of long-term success. The goal isn't to never slip—it's to have a plan for returning when you do. Psychologist Alan Marlatt's work on relapse prevention shows that people who anticipate setbacks and create return strategies are far more likely to sustain change than those who assume they'll never falter. **The key insight: slipping is not failure. Staying away is failure.**
Studies show that the gap between when someone drifts and when they return is the best predictor of long-term maintenance. The faster you return, the more likely the behavior will stick.

Your Return Plan

When you drift (not "if"—_when_), you'll need answers to these questions:

* **What will remind me that I've drifted?**
  A specific day of the week to check in? A trusted person who notices? A calendar reminder?

* **What's the smallest action I can take to return?**
  Not the full ritual—the two-minute version. The baseline from Week 41.

* **Who can I reach out to for support?**
  Not for judgment—for gentle accountability.

* **What mindset will help me come back without shame?**
  Remember Week 9: compassion, not criticism. One miss doesn't erase months of work.

THIS WEEK'S FOCUS

→ **Write your "Return Plan" - so you have it for the next time you lose your way.**
Include also why this mattered to you. What you've already proven you can do. How to return without judgment. That drifting is part of the process, not proof of failure.

→ **Save it somewhere accessible: in your phone, on a sticky note, in this book.**

→ **Commit to the "never miss twice" principle.**
One miss is life. Two misses are a pattern forming. Return quickly.

PROGRESS TRACKER

GOAL # 1
RITUALS:
....
Scheduled for:
....
Accomplished:
....

GOAL # 2
RITUALS:
....
Scheduled for:
....
Accomplished:
....

GOAL # 3
RITUALS:
....
Scheduled for:
....
Accomplished:
....

★THIS WEEK'S INSIGHTS AND LEARNINGS★

What did this week teach me?
....

What's one achievement I'm proud of?
....

What's one thing I'll adjust next week?
....

WEEK 47: STRENGTHENING TRUST
THE FOUNDATION YOU'VE BUILT

You've created a return plan for when you drift. You've acknowledged that setbacks are part of the journey, not evidence of failure. Now, let's talk about something else, something fundamental you've built over the past months —something that can't be taken away, even when you drift: You've built trust in yourself.

Remember early on when trust felt fragile? When you weren't sure if you could rely on yourself to follow through? When every missed day felt like proof that you'd quit eventually? By now, that's changed.

The Research: Self-Trust and Long-Term Change

Psychologist Erik Erikson identified trust as the foundation of psychological development from infants to adults. Self-trust—the belief that you will keep promises to yourself—is equally critical.

Research on self-regulation shows that people with high self-trust experience less internal conflict, lower stress, and greater follow-through on goals. Why? Because they've gathered evidence over time that they'll show up for themselves.

Studies on commitment and consistency reveal that every time you keep a small promise that you made to yourself, you strengthen the neural pathway associated with trustworthiness. Over time, self-trust becomes a self-fulfilling prophecy.

What Builds Trust? Showing Up.

You've shown up—imperfectly, inconsistently sometimes, but repeatedly—for forty-seven weeks. That's not luck. That's integrity. That's evidence. And now, when you commit to something new, a part of you already knows: "I can do this. I've proven it." That quiet confidence is self-trust. And it's one of the most valuable things you've built.

THIS WEEK'S FOCUS

→ Reflect: How has my relationship with myself changed over the past weeks?
Do you trust yourself more now than you did in Week 1? What evidence do you have?

→ Acknowledge one promise you've kept to yourself this year.
Maybe it's showing up for a ritual. Maybe it's returning after missing. Maybe it's adjusting without quitting.

→ Recognize that this foundation is permanent.
Even if you drift, this trust doesn't disappear. You've proven you're someone who returns. That's who you are now.

PROGRESS TRACKER

GOAL # 1
RITUALS:
....
Scheduled for:
....
Accomplished:
....

GOAL # 2
RITUALS:
....
Scheduled for:
....
Accomplished:
....

GOAL # 3
RITUALS:
....
Scheduled for:
....
Accomplished:
....

THIS WEEK'S INSIGHTS AND LEARNINGS

What did this week teach me?
....

What's one achievement I'm proud of?
....

What's one thing I'll adjust next week?
....

WEEK 48: BUILDING ON THIS FOUNDATION
WHAT'S NEXT?

You've built self-trust. You've created a return plan. You've recognized how your growth has rippled outward. By now, a question naturally arises: what comes after this book ends?

The structure that's held you for nearly a year is about to shift. The weekly prompts will stop. The milestone reflections will be completed. The framework that guided you will close. But here's what doesn't end: you.

The Research: Self-Efficacy and Autonomy

Psychologist Albert Bandura's research on self-efficacy shows that confidence in your ability to succeed comes from four sources—but the most powerful one is "mastery experience." You believe you can do something because you've already done it.

Research on autonomy and intrinsic motivation shows that sustainable change happens when external structures fade and internal commitment takes over. The scaffolding was necessary—but now, the structure is inside you.

You Now Know How to Grow

You've shown up for forty-eight weeks. You've built rituals. You've navigated setbacks. You've returned after missing. You've proven to yourself that you can sustain growth. That proof is permanent. It doesn't disappear when the book ends.

This year taught you:

- *How to identify what matters to you - and why!*
- *How to break big goals into manageable rituals*
- *How to start small and build consistency*
- *How to navigate resistance, plateaus, and setbacks*
- *How to return without shame*
- *How to recognize and own your growth*
- *... and so much more. Just take a moment to flip through the Progress Tracker pages!*

These aren't skills that expire. They're skills for life.

THIS WEEK'S FOCUS

→ Take a mindful moment to enjoy how far you've come on this journey.
All these weeks of progress. How does this make you feel?

→ Do you already have something new in mind you want to work on next?
Acknowledge that you're not going to start from scratch. You built a lasting skillset that will kick-start your next season.

PROGRESS TRACKER

GOAL # 1
RITUALS:
....
Scheduled for:
....
Accomplished:
....

GOAL # 2
RITUALS:
....
Scheduled for:
....
Accomplished:
....

GOAL # 3
RITUALS:
....
Scheduled for:
....
Accomplished:
....

THIS WEEK'S INSIGHTS AND LEARNINGS

What did this week teach me?
....

What's one achievement I'm proud of?
....

What's one thing I'll adjust next week?
....

Week 49: The Wisdom of Imperfection
What Your Setbacks Taught You

You've recognized that the skills you've built are permanent. You're ready to continue growing beyond this book. Before you move forward, let's look back at something most people try to forget: the moments when things didn't go as planned.

The weeks you missed. The rituals that felt impossible. The days you wanted to quit. The times you felt like you were failing. Are we opening old wounds? No. We're reframing setbacks as lessons. They weren't obstacles to your growth. They were part of it.

The Research: Learning From Adversity

Psychologists Richard Tedeschi and Lawrence Calhoun developed the concept of **"post-traumatic growth"**—the idea that people can experience profound positive change as a result of struggling with difficult circumstances. Their research shows that adversity often leads to **five types of growth**: *greater appreciation for life, closer relationships, increased personal strength, recognition of new possibilities, and spiritual development.*

Studies on learning and adaptation reveal that setbacks create something success never can: information on how to improve. When something doesn't work, you learn what needs to change. When something feels impossible, you discover what actually matters.

Research by psychologist Carol Dweck shows that people with a growth mindset view setbacks as feedback, not failure. Each struggle becomes a teacher, not a verdict.

What Your Imperfection Taught You

Think back over the past forty-nine weeks. Not at what went perfectly—at what didn't. What did those struggles reveal? What did you learn about yourself that success could never have taught you?

- *Maybe you learned your limits—and how to work with them instead of against them.*
- *Perhaps you discovered what truly matters when everything else falls away.*
- *Or, maybe you found compassion for yourself you didn't know you had.*

These imperfections didn't ruin your journey. They helped you evolve as a result.

This Week's Focus

→ **Identify one setback from this year that taught you something valuable.**
What did that struggle reveal about what you need, what you value, or who you are?

→ **Write what you would tell your "Week-1-Self "about the value of struggling.**
What would you want that earlier version of you to know about imperfection?

→ **Acknowledge that your setbacks made you stronger.** They taught you resilience, self-compassion, and adaptability in a way success alone never could.

PROGRESS TRACKER

GOAL # 1
RITUALS:

....

Scheduled for:

....

Accomplished:

....

GOAL # 2
RITUALS:

....

Scheduled for:

....

Accomplished:

....

GOAL # 3
RITUALS:

....

Scheduled for:

....

Accomplished:

....

★THIS WEEK'S INSIGHTS AND LEARNINGS★

What did this week teach me?

....

What's one achievement I'm proud of?

....

What's one thing I'll adjust next week?

....

WEEK 50: SIMPLIFYING YOUR PRACTICE
WHAT CAN YOU LET GO OF?

You've acknowledged what your setbacks taught you. You've recognized that struggle deepened your growth in ways success alone couldn't. As you approach the final weeks of this journey, it's time to ask a different question: What *doesn't* need to continue?

Back in Week 40, you released what no longer served you—old beliefs, outdated identities, limiting patterns. That was about letting go of the past. This week is different. This is about the present: which rituals have served their purpose? Which practices were meant only for this season? Not everything you built needs to come with you forever.

The Research: The Power of Subtraction

Research by behavioral scientist Leidy Klotz reveals a fascinating pattern: when solving problems, **humans instinctively add rather than subtract**. We think about what more we can do, rarely about what we can remove. But studies show that subtraction—removing what's unnecessary—often leads to better outcomes than addition. Less complexity. More focus. Greater sustainability.

Author Greg McKeown's research on essentialism supports this: the disciplined pursuit of less creates space for what truly matters. When you try to maintain everything, you dilute your energy. When you simplify, you strengthen what remains.

What's Complete?

Some rituals were meant to last a lifetime. Others were meant to teach you something specific—and now that the lesson is learned, it's time to let them go.

- *Maybe a ritual helped you build discipline, and now that discipline is integrated.*
- *Maybe a practice served a particular goal that's complete.*
- *Maybe something felt essential six months ago, but no longer aligns with who you are now.*

Letting go of a ritual doesn't mean it failed. On the contrary, it's proof that it succeeded in what it was meant to do.

THIS WEEK'S FOCUS

→ **Review your current rituals. Ask: "Does this still serve who I'm becoming?"**

→ **Identify one ritual that's complete. Release it with gratitude.**

→ **Simplify to strengthen. By letting go of what's no longer essential, you create space and energy for what truly matters moving forward.**

→ **Remember: You're not abandoning your growth. You're refining it.**

PROGRESS TRACKER

GOAL # 1
RITUALS:
....
Scheduled for:
....
Accomplished:
....

GOAL # 2
RITUALS:
....
Scheduled for:
....
Accomplished:
....

GOAL # 3
RITUALS:
....
Scheduled for:
....
Accomplished:
....

✦ THIS WEEK'S INSIGHTS AND LEARNINGS ✦

What did this week teach me?
....

What's one achievement I'm proud of?
....

What's one thing I'll adjust next week?
....

WEEK 51: YOUR HOPES FOR THE FUTURE
LOOKING FORWARD WITH INTENTION

You've honored what your struggles taught you. You've simplified your practice. You've released what's complete. And now, here you are: the final full week of this journey. Next week, you'll complete your 100% milestone reflection and step beyond the framework that's held you for the past year.

But before you do, it's time to look forward—not with pressure or rigid plans, but with gentle intention. Not "What should I do next?" but "What do I genuinely hope for?"

The Research: Hope and Goal-Directed Behavior

Psychologist Charles Snyder's research on hope theory shows that hope is not wishful thinking—it's a cognitive process that involves both goals (what you want) and pathways (how you'll get there).
Studies show that people with high hope are more resilient, more motivated, and more likely to achieve long-term goals. But hope isn't about optimism alone—it's about believing you have both the will and the way.

What Feels Alive in You?

You've spent fifty weeks proving you have the way. You know how to plant seeds, nurture growth, navigate setbacks, and sustain what you build. Now it's about reconnecting with your intention: what do you genuinely want for your future?

This isn't about creating a new 52-week plan right away or breaking down the rituals that get you there. It's not even about setting ambitious goals or committing to major changes.

It's simply about asking: "What am I curious about? What new paths seem interesting to explore? What do I want to invite more of in my life in the future?"

THIS WEEK'S FOCUS

→ **Complete this sentence:**

"In the year ahead, I am curious to _____ **"**

Let it be honest. Let it be yours.
Don't worry about whether it's ambitious enough or realistic enough.
Just notice what calls you.

Whatever you choose next, you're not starting from scratch.
You're building on one year of proof that you can sustain change.

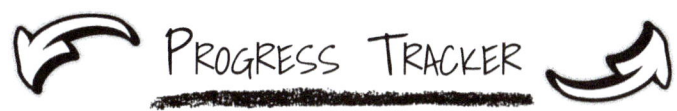

PROGRESS TRACKER

GOAL # 1
RITUALS:

Scheduled for:

Accomplished:

GOAL # 2
RITUALS:

Scheduled for:

Accomplished:

GOAL # 3
RITUALS:

Scheduled for:

Accomplished:

★ THIS WEEK'S INSIGHTS AND LEARNINGS ★

What did this week teach me?

What's one achievement I'm proud of?

What's one thing I'll adjust next week?

100% MILESTONE REFLECTION
THIS IS YOUR ONE YEAR FROM YESTERDAY

Let's talk about what you've accomplished.

Fifty-two weeks ago, you opened this book and imagined yourself one year in the future — living as the person who followed through. The person who stayed consistent. Who kept showing up. You closed your eyes, felt that vision deeply, and promised your future self you'd get here.
And here you are.
Take a moment to let that sink in. How do you feel — proud, grounded, maybe even a little surprised by how far you've come? You should. You earned this.

You did something rare and extraordinary.
You showed up — not perfectly, but persistently. Through motivation and doubt, through momentum and pause. You kept going.
You kept your promise. And that's something to be deeply proud of.
Fewer than 1% of people who set resolutions make it to Week 52 with sustained engagement. You're no longer part of the 99% who stopped. You're part of the 1% who stayed—not because of luck, but because of the choices you made, one day, one week, one season at a time.

What Separates the 1%

Psychologists have studied long-term goal achievers for decades. The findings are consistent:

- They **use systems, not motivation**. *The 1% don't rely on feeling inspired. They build structures that make the right choice easier.*
- They **normalize setbacks**. *They don't interpret missing once as failure. They see it as data. They return quickly, without shame.*
- They **measure progress by consistency, not outcomes**. *They know that showing up matters more than performing perfectly.*
- They've **shifted their identity**. *They no longer see themselves as "trying to become" someone new. They recognize they already are that person.*

You've done all of this. And that's why you're still here. You made it!

This final reflection is different from the others. This isn't about preparing for the next season—it's about honoring the full journey you've completed. Complete the following 5 steps one last time.

Step 1: Review Your Goals and Milestones

Go back to the **goals**. For each one, ask yourself:

- *Did this goal evolve over the year?*
- *What did I actually achieve—beyond what I expected?*
- What surprised me most about this journey?

Goal #1

Goal #2

Goal #3

Now look at your **milestones** for each.

- *Did you achieve them?*
- *Exceed them?*
- *Fall short?*

All outcomes provide valuable learning. If you exceeded expectations, consider setting a higher target for the next season. If you fell short, ask yourself why—and whether your next milestone needs to be more realistic.

Goal #1: 100% Milestone	☐ *achieved*	☐ *exceeded*	☐ *fell short*
Goal #2: 100% Milestone	☐ *achieved*	☐ *exceeded*	☐ *fell short*
Goal #3: 100% Milestone	☐ *achieved*	☐ *exceeded*	☐ *fell short*

Step 2: Identify the Patterns That Serve You in the Future

You've gathered a total of 52 weeks of data about yourself. Did your rhythm evolve over time, or was it more or less consistent? A final reflection will help you build momentum moving forward whenever you need it again!

When do you show up most consistently?
Time of day, day of week, circumstances?

When do you struggle most?
What triggers make it harder?

What helps you return after missing?
What Mindset, strategy, or support gets you back on track?

Step 3: Define What You'll Carry Forward

This book has been your structure for 52 weeks. Now it's time to decide what you want to sustain beyond this framework. Which rituals have become non-negotiable parts of who you are?

Goal #1

The ritual(s) that are now part of my life:

Goal #2:

The ritual(s) that are now part of my life:

Goal #3:

The ritual(s) that are now part of my life:

Step 4: Acknowledge Your Wins

Write at least five things you're genuinely proud of from the past year. Go beyond the obvious achievements. What internal shifts happened? What moments of resilience? What quiet victories that only you know about?

Step 5: Set One Intention for the Next Season

This book ends, but your journey doesn't. The rituals you've built, the identity you've claimed, the patterns you've changed—these continue. What's one thing you want to focus on as you move forward?

Examples:

- *"I want to plant a new seed now that I know how to sustain growth."*
- *"I want to share what I've learned with someone who's just starting."*
- *"I want to trust that I don't need a framework anymore—I've become the structure."*

My intention for the future

Stay Connected

You've made it to Week 52!
Care to share your story, your wins, your reflections?
I'd love to hear how *One Year from Yesterday* helped you grow.
Write a review and help others embark on their growth journey!

If this book has meant something to you, spread the love and give the gift of growth.

Get a copy of *One Year from Yesterday* for your friends and family.

Enroll to the KOMMOR newsletter to hear about updates and promotions.

LETTER FROM THE AUTHOR
YOU DID SOMETHING TRULY EXTRAORDINARY

Dear Reader,

You committed to something most people never finish — not just a goal, but a full year of showing up for your growth. Week by week, you built rituals, navigated setbacks, and kept moving forward — even when things felt slow, uncertain, or invisible.

That takes more than discipline. It takes courage. Compassion. And deep trust in yourself.

Not every week went as planned — that's life. But you kept returning, without shame or perfectionism. You stayed connected to the process, and in doing so, you built something lasting: momentum, self-awareness, and the quiet confidence of someone who doesn't quit on themselves.

That's what One Year from Yesterday was always meant to be — not a rulebook, but a companion. A guide to help you stay grounded in what matters, and to remind you that growth isn't about doing more — it's about doing what's meaningful, with consistency and care.

So keep going. Keep choosing your next steps with intention. Keep becoming.

Your story is still unfolding — and you're exactly where you need to be.

With gratitude and celebration,

Alexandra

Founder of KOMMOR Consulting

References

Amabile, T. M., & Kramer, S. J. (2011). The power of small wins. Harvard Business Review, 89(5), 70–80.

Amabile, T., & Kramer, S. (2011). The progress principle: Using small wins to ignite joy, engagement, and creativity at work. Harvard Business Review Press.

Bandura, A. (1977). Social learning theory. Prentice Hall.

Bandura, A. (1986). Social foundations of thought and action: A social cognitive theory. Prentice Hall.

Bandura, A. (1997). Self-efficacy: The exercise of control. Freeman.

Baumeister, R. F., & Tierney, J. (2011). Willpower: Rediscovering the greatest human strength. Penguin Press.

Bem, D. J. (1972). Self-perception theory. In L. Berkowitz (Ed.), Advances in experimental so-cial psychology (Vol. 6, pp. 1–62). Academic Press. https://doi.org/10.1016/S0065-2601(08)60024-6

Bompa, T. O., & Haff, G. G. (2009). Periodization: Theory and methodology of training (5th ed.). Human Kinetics.

Brailsford, D. (2012). Marginal gains. In Team Sky: How to win the Tour de France. Referenced in Clear, J. (2018). Atomic habits. Avery.

Brandstätter, V., Herrmann, M., & Schüler, J. (2013). The struggle of giving up personal goals: Affective, physiological, and cognitive consequences of an action crisis. Personality and Social Psychology Bulletin, 39(12), 1668–1682. https://doi.org/10.1177/0146167213500151

Brown, B. (2010). The gifts of imperfection: Let go of who you think you're supposed to be and embrace who you are. Hazelden.

Charney, D. S. (2004). Psychobiological mechanisms of resilience and vulnerability: Implications for successful adaptation to extreme stress. American Journal of Psychiatry, 161(2), 195–216. https://doi.org/10.1176/appi.ajp.161.2.195

Christakis, N. A., & Fowler, J. H. (2007). The spread of obesity in a large social network over 32 years. New England Journal of Medicine, 357(4), 370–379. https://doi.org/10.1056/NEJMsa066082

Christakis, N. A., & Fowler, J. H. (2009). Connected: The surprising power of our social networks and how they shape our lives. Little, Brown and Company.

Clance, P. R., & Imes, S. A. (1978). The imposter phenomenon in high achieving women: Dynamics and therapeutic intervention. Psychotherapy: Theory, Research & Practice, 15(3), 241–247. https://doi.org/10.1037/h0086006

Clear, J. (2018). Atomic habits: An easy & proven way to build good habits & break bad ones. Avery.

Cohen, G. L., & Sherman, D. K. (2014). The psychology of change: Self-affirmation and social psychological intervention. Annual Review of Psychology, 65, 333–371. https://doi.org/10.1146/annurev-psych-010213-115137

Csikszentmihalyi, M. (1990). Flow: The psychology of optimal experience. Harper & Row.

Csikszentmihalyi, M. (1997). Finding flow: The psychology of engagement with everyday life. Basic Books.

David, S. (2016). Emotional agility: Get unstuck, embrace change, and thrive in work and life. Avery.

Deci, E. L., & Ryan, R. M. (1985). Intrinsic motivation and self-determination in human behav-ior. Plenum Press.

Deci, E. L., & Ryan, R. M. (2000). The "what" and "why" of goal pursuits: Human needs and the self-determination of behavior. Psychological Inquiry, 11(4), 227–268. https://doi.org/10.1207/S15327965PLI1104_01

Dement, W. C., & Vaughan, C. (1999). The promise of sleep: A pioneer in sleep medicine ex-plores the vital connection between health, happiness, and a good night's sleep. Dell Pub-lishing.

Dewey, J. (1933). How we think: A restatement of the relation of reflective thinking to the educa-tive process. D. C. Heath.

Duckworth, A. (2016). Grit: The power of passion and perseverance. Scribner.

Duhigg, C. (2012). The power of habit: Why we do what we do in life and business. Random House.

Dweck, C. S. (2006). Mindset: The new psychology of success. Random House.

Dweck, C. S., Walton, G. M., & Cohen, G. L. (2014). Academic tenacity: Mindsets and skills that promote long-term learning. Bill & Melinda Gates Foundation.

Eldredge, N., & Gould, S. J. (1972). Punctuated equilibria: An alternative to phyletic gradu-alism. In T. J. M. Schopf (Ed.), Models in paleobiology (pp. 82–115). Freeman Cooper.

Emmons, R. A. (2007). Thanks! How the new science of gratitude can make you happier. Houghton Mifflin.

Emmons, R. A., & McCullough, M. E. (2003). Counting blessings versus burdens: An ex-peri-mental investigation of gratitude and subjective well-being in daily life. Journal of Per-sonality and Social Psychology, 84(2), 377–389. https://doi.org/10.1037/0022-3514.84.2.377

Ericsson, K. A. (2006). The influence of experience and deliberate practice on the de-velopment of superior expert performance. In K. A. Ericsson, N. Charness, P. J. Feltovich, & R. R. Hoffman (Eds.), The Cambridge handbook of expertise and expert performance (pp. 683–703). Cambridge University Press. https://doi.org/10.1017/CBO9780511816796.038

Ericsson, K. A., & Pool, R. (2016). Peak: Secrets from the new science of expertise. Houghton Mifflin Harcourt.

Ericsson, K. A., Krampe, R. T., & Tesch-Römer, C. (1993). The role of deliberate practice in the acquisition of expert performance. Psychological Review, 100(3), 363–406. https://doi.org/10.1037/0033-295X.100.3.363

Erikson, E. H. (1950). Childhood and society. W. W. Norton & Company.

Erikson, E. H. (1968). Identity: Youth and crisis. W. W. Norton & Company.

Festinger, L. (1954). A theory of social comparison processes. Human Relations, 7(2), 117–140. https://doi.org/10.1177/001872675400700202

Fishbach, A., & Koo, M. (2012). Dynamics of self-regulation: How (un)accomplished goal ac-tions affect motivation. In R. M. Ryan (Ed.), The Oxford handbook of human moti-vation (pp. 70–93). Oxford University Press.

Fishbach, A., & Tu, Y. (2016). When wishing upon a star doesn't help: Highlighting the ne-cessity of goal pursuit. Personality and Social Psychology Bulletin, 42(7), 877–893. https://doi.org/10.1177/0146167216650169

Fogg, B. J. (2009). A behavior model for persuasive design. Proceedings of the 4th International Conference on Persuasive Technology. https://doi.org/10.1145/1541948.1541999

Fogg, B. J. (2020). Tiny habits: The small changes that change everything. Houghton Mifflin Harcourt.

Frederick, S., & Loewenstein, G. (1999). Hedonic adaptation. In D. Kahneman, E. Diener, & N. Schwarz (Eds.), Well-being: The foundations of hedonic psychology (pp. 302–329). Rus-sell Sage Foundation.

Goffman, E. (1959). The presentation of self in everyday life. Anchor Books.

Gollwitzer, P. M. (1999). Implementation intentions: Strong effects of simple plans. American Psychologist, 54(7), 493–503. https://doi.org/10.1037/0003-066X.54.7.493

Gollwitzer, P. M., & Sheeran, P. (2006). Implementation intentions and goal achievement: A me-ta-analysis of effects and processes. Advances in Experimental Social Psychology, 38, 69–119. https://doi.org/10.1016/S0065-2601(06)38002-1

Grant, A. M. (2003). The impact of life coaching on goal attainment, metacognition, and mental health. Social Behavior and Personality: An International Journal, 31(3), 253–264. https://doi.org/10.2224/sbp.2003.31.3.253

Harkin, B., Webb, T. L., Chang, B. P. I., Prestwich, A., Conner, M., Kellar, I., Benn, Y., & Sheeran, P. (2016). Does monitoring goal progress promote goal attainment? A meta-analysis of the experimental evidence. Psychological Bulletin, 142(2), 198–229. https://doi.org/10.1037/bul0000025

Hayes, S. C., Luoma, J. B., Bond, F. W., Masuda, A., & Lillis, J. (2006). Acceptance and com-mitment therapy: Model, processes and outcomes. Behaviour Research and Therapy, 44(1), 1–25. https://doi.org/10.1016/j.brat.2005.06.006

Hayes, S. C., Strosahl, K. D., & Wilson, K. G. (2011). Acceptance and commitment therapy: The process and practice of mindful change (2nd ed.). Guilford Press.

Hendricks, G. (2009). The big leap: Conquer your hidden fear and take life to the next level. HarperOne.

Hewitt, P. L., & Flett, G. L. (1991). Perfectionism in the self and social contexts: Conceptuali-za-tion, assessment, and association with psychopathology. Journal of Personality and Social Psychology, 60(3), 456–470. https://doi.org/10.1037/0022-3514.60.3.456

James, W. (1890). The principles of psychology (Vol. 1). Henry Holt and Company.

Kahneman, D. (2011). Thinking, fast and slow. Farrar, Straus and Giroux.

Kahneman, D., & Tversky, A. (1979). Prospect theory: An analysis of decision under risk. Econ-ometrica, 47(2), 263–291. https://doi.org/10.2307/1914185

Kashdan, T. B., & Rottenberg, J. (2010). Psychological flexibility as a fundamental aspect of health. Clinical Psychology Review, 30(7), 865–878. https://doi.org/10.1016/j.cpr.2010.03.001

Kleitman, N. (1963). Sleep and wakefulness (Rev. ed.). University of Chicago Press.

Kolb, D. A. (1984). Experiential learning: Experience as the source of learning and development. Prentice Hall.

Koo, M., & Fishbach, A. (2012). The small-area hypothesis: Effects of progress monitoring on goal adherence. Journal of Consumer Research, 39(3), 493–509. https://doi.org/10.1086/663827

Lally, P., van Jaarsveld, C. H. M., Potts, H. W. W., & Wardle, J. (2010). How are habits formed: Modelling habit formation in the real world. European Journal of Social Psychology, 40(6), 998–1009. https://doi.org/10.1002/ejsp.674

Langer, E. J. (1989). Mindfulness. Addison-Wesley.

Langer, E. J. (2014). The power of mindful learning (2nd ed.). Da Capo Press.

Langer, E. J., & Moldoveanu, M. (2000). The construct of mindfulness. Journal of Social Issues, 56(1), 1–9. https://doi.org/10.1111/0022-4537.00148

LeDoux, J. E. (2015). Anxious: Using the brain to understand and treat fear and anxiety. Viking.

Levinson, D. J. (1978). The seasons of a man's life. Knopf.

Levinson, D. J. (1996). The seasons of a woman's life. Knopf.

Lieberman, M. D. (2013). Social: Why our brains are wired to connect. Crown Publishers.

Locke, E. A., & Latham, G. P. (2002). Building a practically useful theory of goal setting and task motivation: A 35-year odyssey. American Psychologist, 57(9), 705–717. https://doi.org/10.1037/0003-066X.57.9.705

Marlatt, G. A., & Gordon, J. R. (1985). Relapse prevention: Maintenance strategies in the treatment of addictive behaviors. Guilford Press

Marlatt, G. A., & Donovan, D. M. (Eds.). (2005). Relapse prevention: Maintenance strategies in the treatment of addictive behaviors (2nd ed.). Guilford Press.

Maslow, A. H. (1954). Motivation and personality. Harper & Row.

Maslow, A. H. (1968). Toward a psychology of being (2nd ed.). Van Nostrand.

McAdams, D. P. (2001). The psychology of life stories. Review of General Psychology, 5(2), 100–122. https://doi.org/10.1037/1089-2680.5.2.100

McAdams, D. P. (2008). Personal narratives and the life story. In O. P. John, R. W. Robins, & L. A. Pervin (Eds.), Handbook of personality: Theory and research (3rd ed., pp. 242–262). Guilford Press.

McAdams, D. P., & McLean, K. C. (2013). Narrative identity. Current Directions in Psychologi-cal Science, 22(3), 233–238. https://doi.org/10.1177/0963721413475622

Mednick, S. C., Nakayama, K., & Stickgold, R. (2003). Sleep-dependent learning: A nap is as good as a night. Nature Neuroscience, 6(7), 697–698. https://doi.org/10.1038/nn1078

Neff, K. D. (2003). Self-compassion: An alternative conceptualization of a healthy attitude to-ward oneself. Self and Identity, 2(2), 85–101. https://doi.org/10.1080/15298860309032

Neff, K. D. (2011). Self-compassion: The proven power of being kind to yourself. William Mor-row.

Newell, A., & Rosenbloom, P. S. (1981). Mechanisms of skill acquisition and the law of practice. In J. R. Anderson (Ed.), Cognitive skills and their acquisition (pp. 1–55). Lawrence Erl-baum Associates.

Norcross, J. C., & Vangarelli, D. J. (1988). The resolution solution: Longitudinal examination of New Year's change attempts. Journal of Substance Abuse, 1(2), 127–134. https://doi.org/10.1016/S0899-3289(88)80016-6

Norcross, J. C., Mrykalo, M. S., & Blagys, M. D. (2002). Auld lang Syne: Success predictors, change processes, and self-reported outcomes of New Year's resolvers and non-resolvers. Journal of Clinical Psychology, 58(4), 397–405. https://doi.org/10.1002/jclp.1151

Oyserman, D., Bybee, D., & Terry, K. (2006). Possible selves and academic outcomes: How and when possible selves impel action. Journal of Personality and Social Psychology, 91(1), 188–204. https://doi.org/10.1037/0022-3514.91.1.188

Prochaska, J. O., & DiClemente, C. C. (1983). Stages and processes of self-change of smoking: Toward an integrative model of change. Journal of Consulting and Clinical Psychology, 51(3), 390–395. https://doi.org/10.1037/0022-006X.51.3.390

Prochaska, J. O., & Velicer, W. F. (1997). The transtheoretical model of health behavior change. American Journal of Health Promotion, 12(1), 38–48. https://doi.org/10.4278/0890-1171-12.1.38

Prochaska, J. O., Redding, C. A., & Evers, K. E. (2015). The transtheoretical model and stages of change. In K. Glanz, B. K. Rimer, & K. Viswanath (Eds.), Health behavior: Theory, re-search, and practice (5th ed., pp. 125–148). Jossey-Bass.

Rossi, E. L., & Nimmons, D. (1991). The 20-minute break: Using the new science of ultradian rhythms. Tarcher/Putnam.

Ryan, R. M., & Deci, E. L. (2017). Self-determination theory: Basic psychological needs in mo-tivation, development, and wellness. Guilford Press.

Schultz, W. (2015). Neuronal reward and decision signals: From theories to data. Physiological Reviews, 95(3), 853–951. https://doi.org/10.1152/physrev.00023.2014

Schön, D. A. (1983). The reflective practitioner: How professionals think in action. Basic Books.

Seligman, M. E. P. (2011). Flourish: A visionary new understanding of happiness and well-being. Free Press.

Snyder, C. R. (2002). Hope theory: Rainbows in the mind. Psychological Inquiry, 13(4), 249–275. https://doi.org/10.1207/S15327965PLI1304_01

Snyder, C. R., Irving, L. M., & Anderson, J. R. (1991). Hope and health. In C. R. Snyder & D. R. Forsyth (Eds.), Handbook of social and clinical psychology: The health perspective (pp. 285–305). Pergamon Press.